Quaker Minutes of the Eastern Shore of Maryland

1676-1779

Third Haven and Cecil Monthly Meetings

F. Edward Wright

Colonial Roots
Millsboro, DE
2014

ISBN 978-1-68034-016-7

Printed in the United States of America
Third printing 2014

CONTENTS

INTRODUCTION

Third Haven Monthly Meeting

Quakerism probably first reached the Eastern Shore of Maryland at Kent Island but its center soon shifted inland with the establishment of Third Haven Meeting in Talbot County.

George Fox spent a few days in Talbot County on his first visit in 1672 where he attended a General Meeting "near Great Choptank River." Later the same year Fox returned to Talbot County at which time he visited Robert Harwood at Miles River and attended another General Meeting at Betty's Cove, lasting five days. In his journals Fox sensed an increased respectability for his movement in Maryland, noting "many people of account" were now attending the meetings.

Following Fox's visit and those of Burnyeat and Edmondson, Quakerism on the Eastern Shore went into a period of great growth. By 1677 there were meetings at Betty's Cove, Choptank (southern Talbot County), Bayside (Talbot County) Tuckahoe (Kings Creek, Talbot County), Kent Island, Little Choptank (Dorcester County) and Annamessex (Somerset county). Within a few years there were additional meetings at Sassafras and Chester. Third Haven Meeting House in present-day Easton was completed in 1685. Betty's Cove Meeting was removed to Third Haven in 1693.

In Dorchester County there were two notable meetings, Little Choptank (Fishing Creek) and Transquaking Meeting. The former appeared in the records of Third Haven Monthly Meeting in 1687; it had disappeared by the 1750s. Transquaking Meeting was probably formed in the late 1690s; it was discontinued in 1748.

The microfilm holdings of the Maryland State Archives cover the following early records of Third Haven Monthly Meeting: Births, 1664-1929: M284; Burials, 1672-1952: M284; Marriages, 1668-1935: M286; Certificate of removal, 1798-1914: M285; Minutes, 1676-1871: M283, 284, 288; Women's minutes, 1705-1760, 1770-1879: M285, 288.

Cecil Monthly Meeting

In 1698 the meetings of Cecil and Chester meetings were separated from Third Haven Monthly Meeting and formed as Cecil Monthly Meeting. Cecil Meeting was located near the town of Lynch, in what is now Kent County. The meeting house was built prior to 1694. Chester Meeting was formed as early as 1679 and was comprised of Friends living near Chester River in Queen Anne's County. Further north was Sassafras

Meeting, formed prior to 1679 on the Sassafras River. By 1689 it was nearly extinct and soon disappeared from the records.

As was the case of Third Haven not all the marriages of Cecil Monthly Meeting were recorded in the registers and hence the minutes offer a means to fill in some of these omissions.

The records of the register of Cecil Monthly Meeting have been abstracted and published in Part III of the Appendix of Carroll's *Quakerism on the Eastern Shore* and in the *Maryland Eastern Shore Vital Records* series. The microfilm holdings of MSA include the following reels for the earlier periods: Register, 1678-1913: M980; Marriages, 1698-1784, 1788-1851: M908; Minutes, 1698-1840: M909, 910; women's minutes, 1765-1848:M909.

Marriages omitted from the Registers

The minutes show that many marriages were not recorded in the registers. I have identified these marriages by an asterisk or asterisks. A single asterisk indicates that a report was made that the marriage had been "orderly accomplished." A double asterisk indicates that although the couple had announced their intentions a first and second time with the approval of the meeting to proceed in marriage, the minutes do not record that the marriage had been "orderly accomplished" - probably an unintended omission. A triple asterisk indicates that only the initial declaration of intent is recorded in the minutes. When the marriage was recorded in the register we include the date of marriage in brackets, following the entry as abstracted from the minutes. There are also instances when marriages were recorded in the registers but not in the minutes. To get a complete record of marriages one must combine the minutes with the registers. Entries from the registers were published in Kenneth Carroll's *Quakerism on the Eastern Shore* and in F. Edward Wright's *Maryland Eastern Shore Vital Records* series.

Certificates of Removal

Certificates of removal were letters or statements regarding the individual's past conduct; these were sent to the monthly meeting whose verge (general geographical area of the members) encompassed the intended destination of a Quaker. When a Quaker family planned to remove to another area a request was initiated to have a certificate prepared and sent to the future monthly meeting. Collections of copies have survived at many monthly meetings. Copies of the certificates for Third Haven have survived for the period 1798-1914 and for Cecil Monthly Meeting, 1832-1904. Prior to these periods one must rely on the minutes to reveal the requests and preparation of these certificates and hence clues to the movements of Quaker families. Unfortunately the names of family members other than the father, are omitted in many instances.

Other Quaker concerns

Many of the extracts which we have included here obviously reflect events of the time. There are recordings of "sufferings" which refer to confiscation of property for the benefit of the Anglican Church and later for the support of the American Revolution. As the Quaker movement engaged in the riddance of slavery we see the many side issues it presented and the eventual manumission of slaves by members of the society.

Brevity of the abstracts

This book is a collection of entries which reveal information helpful to the genealogist in extending his lineage and acquainting the researcher with events of a personal nature. Omitted are discussions of general concern to the meeting such as poor attendance, repair of buildings, discussion of concerns of the quarterly and yearly meetings, and other subjects of a general nature. To acquire an understanding of the issues faced by our Eastern Shore Quakers and the history of their movement we strongly recommend Kenneth Carroll's *Quakerism on the Eastern Shore.*

I have been as brief and concise (some will say too brief) in extracting the essence of the minutes. It was not the nature of Quakerism to arrive at a judgment or resolution quickly. In ascertaining the nature of a person's "disorder" and getting that person to accept responsibility and to condemn his behavior often took many sessions with members of the Society. To have recorded each entry wherein a particular issue was discussed would have expanded the intended length of this work many fold.

F. Edward Wright
Lewes, Delaware
2001

24/1/1676. Meeting at Wenlock Christisons. Bryan Omealy and John Pitt to oversee the finishing of the meeting house at Bettys Cove.

14/5/1676. Bryon Omealy and Mary Lewis declared their intentions to marry. [They m. 27/6/1676.]

3/9/1676. John Edmondson and Howell Powell to go with John Pitt and Thomas Taylor on 4th day of next week to Ralph Fishbourn's to assist in the dividing the estate belonging to said Ralph and Bryan Omealy.

30/9/1676. George Parrott and Elizabeth Bodwell declared their intentions to marry. [They m. at the house of William Parratt, 3/11/1677.]

30/9/1676. Jane Greenaway dying at Tho: Taylors did before her departure desire that what charge and trouble friends had been at with her in her sickness should be satisfied out of her own things in her trunk.

22/12/1677. To lay before Robert Kemp his disorderly walking.

19/2/1677. Regarding the difference between Bryon Omealia and Ralph Fishbourn [relating to the estate of Wm. Lewis, dec'd.] it was judged that Bryon Omealia in the right of his wife is joyntly and equally concerned with Ra: Fishbourn in the land, as also another tract named Lewis in Michaels River both given and bequeathed by William Lewis dec'd. unto Sarah his wife also since deceased without issue.

19/2/1677. William Berry and Tho: Taylor, execs. of the estate of Richard Preston being concerned for the orphan Samuell Preston and being dissatisfied that the estate is kept from the child.

21/1/1678/9. William Berry, Junr. being intended to goe to Ireland, desired a certificate, with the consent of his father and mother-in-law.

27/10/1678. In as much as Obadiah Judkins and Obedience Jenner did sometime since lay their intents of coming together as husband and wife ... were advised that they should proceed no further till a certificate was procured out of England on the young woman's account, she being but of late come into this country and that they should live apart till the same was effected to which they consented - but she has attempted to have persuade Obadiah to take her contrary to the truth.

27/10/1678. Andrew Orem and Eleanor Morris, daughter of John and Eleanor Morris declared their intentions to marry, she having her parents' consent. [They m. at the house of John Pitts, 21/12/1678.]

17/3/1678. To visit Dennis Hopkins and his wife regarding his woman servant [probably regarding their treatment of her]. The woman servant was examined and Dennis Hopkins and his wife were cleared.

17/3/1678. Charles Gorsuch has taken a wife contrary to the order of truth.

17/3/1678. William Southbee and Joane Lee declared their intentions to marry. [They m. 20/4/1677 at the house of Thomas Taylor in Talbot Co.]

17/3/1678. Thomas Alexander has lost a hogshead of tobacco out of Henry Woolchurch's house.

9/6/1678. Someone from the meeting will visit John Spooner and his wife during their sickness.

9/6/1678. It was agreed that John Pitt shall supply Edward Mosely with leather thred and other necessaries for making of shoes and to pay for the said Moseley's diet at some Friend's house till the next 12th month at which time said Edward Mosely doth ingage himselfe to work journey work for the said Pitt, he allowing him 12 lbs. of tobacco per paire for making men and women's shoes and 2d per pair for cutting out.

6/7/1678. Robert Kemp declared his intents of taking Elizabeth Webb to wife and desired the advice of the meeting and the meeting advised him to forbear for the present.

19/1/1679/80. Richd. Hall and Sarah Rascoe [Rastoe] declared their intentions to marry. [They m. 21/2/1680.]

25/10/1679. Charles Gorsuch stated he intended to remove to Patapsco.

25/10/1679. John Parsons has taken a wife contrary to the order of Truth.

25/10/1679. Wm. Meares and Eliza: Webb declared their intentions to marry. [William Meers of Calvert Co., and Elizabeth Webb of Talbot Co., m. 1/9/1679 at the meeting house at the Tuckahoe meeting house.]

25/10/1679. The widow Ford and her children are in want.

20/12/1679. On behalf of the meeting Wm. Southebee has written to Chester Friends to deal with John Parsons.

20/12/1679. Lovelace Gorsuch laid a matter before the meeting concerning a bond which he hath of Tho: Taylor of Dorchester Co. about the making good a tract of land of 1000 a. which as by his receipt it appears he hath received 15000 lbs. of tobacco.

20/12/1679. The meeting has received satisfaction for Friends of Salem concerning Sarah Hall and therewith fully satisfied, and in as much as Wm. Jones and Sarah Hall have been condescending to the advice of Friends till things were cleared according to the order of Truth, the meeting hath left them to their freedom to come together in marriage.

4/5/1679. The women's meeting signifies a reason to visit the widow Parrott.

8/6/1679. John Gush proffers a paper wherein he is concerned for his brother-in-law John Stacey, servant to the widow [Eliza:] Christerson.

8/6/1679. Lovelate [Lovelace] Gorsuch and Rebeccah Preston declared their intentions to marry. [[They m. 23/8/1679 at the house of Howell Powell.]

31/8/1679. Jacob Abrahams hath produced evidences that he is of age according to the will of his father dec'd., which is 19 years of age - his estate will be delivered to him.

31/8/1679. Emanuell Jenkinson and Eliza. Morgan declared their intentions to marry. [They m. 1/10/1679 at the house of John Edmondson.]

14/9/1679. Wm. Jones and Sarah Hall declared their intentions to marry. On 28/9/1679 Wm. Jones and Sarah Hall were advised not to proceed in marriage till Wm. Jones's wife has been dead a full twelve months. [They m. 24/12/1679 at the house of William Berry.]

14/9/1679. Widow [widow of William] Ford says that she would willingly that her estate might be taken out of Edward Pinder's hands if with conveniency.

28/9/1679. Some lines from Tho: Taylor that the meeting consider of what Jacob Abrahams should allow yearly for his sister's maintenance.

24/10/1680. Benjamin Parrott being kept out of his just due by John Lane who stands indebted to him in the sum of 1400 lbs. of tobacco.

24/10/1680. The meeting to assist and advise Widow Gush in her outward concerns.

7/11/1680. William Sharp desired to be released of the keeping the boate that belongs to the meeting and the meeting agreed. William Sharp intends to go to England.

8/11/1680 (Quarterly meeting). continued with friends' paper from Barbados concerning their proceedings with Robert and Ann Wilson being read.

10/2/1680. Nathaniell Cleeve acquainted the meeting that a daughter of his had lately been stolen away from him and conveyed to James Clayland, priest, who granted them a license and married them all in one day which he said seemed contrary to all just law and reason and the meeting has referred the matter to the half year meeting.

10/2/1680. Obadiah Judkins and Eliza. Barden declared their intentions to marry; the meeting desires that they wait until her husband has been dead twelve months.

10/2/1680. William Dixon and Eliza. Christerson (widow of Winlock) declared their intentions to marry - the meeting will enquire into the welfare of her children. [They m. 8/4/1680 at the home of Elizabeth Cristerson.]

10/2/1680. John West and Jone Beckett declared their intentions to marry. [John West of Cecil Co., and Joan Beerest, formerly of Salem on the Delaware m. 2/3/1680 at Tuckahoe Meeting House.]

10/2/1680. Bartholomew Jadwin and Anne Asdell declared their intentions to marry. [Bartholomew Jadwin and Ann Estell m. 26/4/1680 at the house of John Jadwin.]

19/5/1680. John Pitt and Sarah Thomas of Kent declared their intentions to marry. [John Pitt, planter of Talbot Co., and Sarah Thomas of Kent Co., m. 25/6/1680.]

19/5/1680. Friends at Accomack are not fully satisfied concerning John Parsons' actions whilst he lived there and it was decided that he should goe down to Accomack as soon as possible to answer the truth and give Friends satisfaction.

19/5/1680. An inventory was taken of the estate of Winlock Christerson [and is recorded in the minutes of the meeting.] The goods to be divided betwixt the widow Elizabeth Christerson and her daughter Eliza. Christerson as by will.

6/6/1680. Benjamin Parrott and Elizabeth Keine declared their intentions to marry. [Benjamin Parratt and Elizabeth Keen, both of Talbot Co., m. 21/8/1680.]

3/7/1680. Wm. Dickenson and Elizabeth Powell declared their intentions to marry. [They m. at the house of Howell Powell, 16/10/1680.]

19/8/1680. James Harrisson of Talbot Co. d. and by his will leaving his wife his sole extx.

19/8/1680. Tho: Hutchinson is removed from the house he had of Wm. Stevens, Junr. at Island Creek and also Wm. Stevens having lett out his house and plantation to another, this meeting hath ordered that the Quarterly Meeting be kept att Tho: Hutchinsons where he now liveth.

20/11/1681. Attempts have been made by the meeting to settle those accounts depending between the widow Harrison and Thomas Hutchinson who promised to pay her 3200 lbs. of tobacco but now defers.

16/7/1681. The execs. of Wenlock Christerson being arrested at the suit of Wm. Diggs concerning some Negro sent by Winlock out of Barbadoss to this country by one Edward Ostin.

16/7/1681 (Quarterly meeting). John Spooner sent a paper.

28/8/1681. Obadiah Judkins and Jane Huntington declared their intentions to marry. [Obadiah Judkins and Joan Huntington, both of Talbot Co., m. 4/11/1681 at the house of William Southbee.]

28/8/1681. Dorrothy Hutchinson presented her certificate.

28/8/1681. Michaell Russell and Elisabeth Shaw declared their intentions to marry. Michael Russell also laid before the meeting his out runnings in taking more drink than was needful and also signified his griefe and trouble for the same and desiring the assistance of Friends in order to the clearing of the truth and also his outrunning in letting his mind out after a young woman that comes not amongst Friends and proceeding to marriage. [At the next meeting they renewed their intentions and were given approval.] On 28/8/1689 Michael Russell was visited and he seem to be sorry and ashamed of his outrunnings.

16/1/1682/3. This meeting having an account of Robert and Ann Wilson from the friends of the meeting they belonged unto in old England.

19/11/1682. Tho: Howell intends to remove to Jones on Delaware Bay.

19/11/1682. Wm. Sockwell intends to remove to Jones on Delaware Bay.

19/11/1682. John Keelld was given a cow, he being a poor man and having a charge of children.

19/11/1682. Edward Moseley intends to remove to Jones on Delaware Bay.

19/11/1682. Richard Rattliff, late of Rosendale in Lancashire in old England produced a certificate.

19/11/1682. Tho: Mig... intends to remove to Jones on Delaware Bay.

2/12/1682. Emanuell Jenkinson has an intention to go to England and requests a certificate.

12/3/1682. A certificate on behalf of Stephen Keddy and John Ashdell and his sister Anna and Isabella Harrison and Mary wife of John Keedy from the monthly meeting they belonged unto in England.

26/3/1682. Richard Mitchell appointed to replace John Pitt who is removed from Treadhaven.

26/3/1682. James Barber and Mary Gush declared their intentions to marry. [They m. 18/5/1682.]

26/3/1682. Thomas Furby has gone with his wife and children to a marriage not owned by Friends.

26/3/1682 (Quarterly meeting). The meeting had a real sense of the sad estate and condition of Ralph Elston by his giving way to the enemie of his soul [persisting in a gainsaying spirit and being overtaken in in drink].

10/4/1682. Reported that Margarett Bowes had two severall times given way to an angry spirit and had spoken and acted to the grief of Friends.

24/4/1682 (Quarterly meeting). In as much as Wm. Stevens, Senr. and his son John doe slight the meeting being as their house and bid friends remove it, if they will. This meeting appoints [determines or rules] that the monthly meeting be removed from Wm. Stevens, Senr. to Howell Powell's.

7/5/1682. Peter Willson of Sasifrax and Elisabeth Morgan, daughter in law to Bryon Omealia declared their intentions to marry. [They m. 6/6/1682.]

7/5/1682. Henry Pratt has gone to trayning.

8/5/1682. Stephen Keddy gave his inclination of removing to Chester to settle there.

10/9/1682. John Stacy chose his brother-in-law James Barber for his guardian.

10/9/1682. William Johnson of Rattcliff in old England, mariner, and Sarah Edmondson, daughter of John and Sarah Edmondson, of this Province, declared their intentions to marry. He brought a certificate from Friends and also from his mother. [They m. 26/10/1682.]

24/9/1682. Wm. Berry laid the matter of Samuell Prestons hiring the plantation which his grandfather Preston left him by will, till he came to full age to be possessed with it; a committee to treat with Benjamin Lawrence about the said plantation.

14/1/1683/4. Richard Ratcliff laid his intentions of removing to Jones on

Delaware. A certificate was prepared.

15/12/1683. Wm. Dickenson according to the advice of the last monthly meeting came to this meeting and brought with him original divisions of his father's estate belonging to his brother Walter and sister Rachell Dickenson. [The estate was divided into 4 equal shares. (the inventories of Wm. and Rachell are shown.]

15/12/1683. Thomas Newhouse came to the meeting seeking assistance in persuading his wife to come to him as her place is to do. [She apparently remains behind in Virginia.]

13/2/1683. Solomon Thomas having suddaine occation to goe to old England desires that a certificate might be sent after him.

13/2/1683. A scandalous report has been cast upon Henry Woolchurch by reason of his daughter's [Mary Hackett] having a child in his house (and as by report not by her owne husband).

27/2/1683. Mary Hackett, daughter of Henry Woolchurch has cleared her father from reproach and scandall by confessing the name of the father of her child.

27/2/1683. Solomon Thomas by his sister Sharp [sic] desired a certificate be sent after him to old England by reason the shipp sailed before this meeting.

11/3/1683. A visit to James Hall and his wife found him "very hard and full of reflection upon truth and Friends," laying he did question whether truth were truth or wheather Friends were the people of God or not and that he could find as much peace under a tree att home as att a meeting ..." There was a shew of tenderness and humility in his wife.

8/4/1683. William White of Rappahannock in Lancaster Co., VA, and Martha Smith of the same place, declared their intentions to marry. [They m. 8/4/1683.]

20/5/1683. Isaac Smith, schoolmaster, having lately his residence and employment amongst Friends at Kings Creek and Tuccaho and there falling into distraction of mind having formerly been in the same condition where he lived in Virginia and in this condition being subject to tear and destroy his cloaths and committ other destructive things. Friends thought it the best way to keep him up for the prevention of like things and fearing worse might follow but he being broak away this meetings desires to make inquiry after him and persuade him to go to Friends who would continue their care towards him in order to his being restored to his right mind or if he will not be persuaded then to acquaint the next magistrate.

6/5/1683. Henry Parrott and Mary Bates declared their intentions to marry. [They m. 5/5/1683.]

3/6/1683. Edmond Webb has for sometime absented himself from Friends meetings. When visited he said he never expected to return.

3/6/1683. John Nunam condemned his outrunnings.

28/7/1683. Robert Parrish laid his intention of removing to Joneses on Delaware Bay.

23/9/1683. In as much as Walter Dickenson left his son Wm. his exec., leaving him to the advice and assistance of the men's meeting, the following were appointed to help him: Wm. Berry, John Edmondson, Henry Parrott, Wm. Stevens, Wm. Sharp, John Pitt and Tho: Taylor.

17/11/1684. Mary Swift, widow, laid her poverty before the meeting; she has great need of a bed. [This was taken care of.]

13/12/1684. Edward Owen and Hannah Baxter declared their intentions to marry. [Edward Owen of Kent in PA and Hannah Baxter m. at the meeting house at Michael's River 15/1/1684.]

13/12/1684. The meeting is well satisfied with those four Friends Tho: Taylor selected to take care of his children and estate.

9/3/1684. John Pemberton and Margarett Mathewes declared their intentions to marry. [John Pemberton of Tuckahoe in Talbot Co. and Margaret Matthews of the same place m. 11/4/1684.]

6/4/1684. A certificate for Wm. Berry, Jr., to Jones Creek on Delaware River.

6/4/1684. James Barber signified to the meeting his shortness in not acquainting Friends with his removal to Chester before he had removed.

1/6/1684. A difference has arisen between Nathaniell Cleeve and Obadiah Judkin with unsavory words spoken.

29/6/1684. Abraham Strand refrains from coming to meetings.

12/7/1684. Solomon Thomas absents himself from meetings.

26/7/1684. Wm. Dixon has in mind selling a Negro his freedom; seeks advice.

21/9/1684. Ralph Swift upon his death bed had a desire to speak with Friends, desiring to buried in Friends Graveyard which was approved.

21/9/1684. James Ridly and Anna Ellitt declared their intentions to marry.

12/1/1685. It is the sense of this meeting that Sarah Jones refrain from the company of Wm. Harriss (who seeks her to wife).

12/1/1685. Wm. Troth and Isabellah Harrisson [widow of James Harrisson] declared their intentions to marry. Committee to meet at the house of Isabella Harrisson to see what she has done or intends to do for her children before her marriage. [They m. 20/2/1685.]

12/1/1685. James Berry and Sarah Woolchurch declared their intentions to marry. [They m. 14/2/1686.]

11/2/1685. Solomon Thomas and Rebeccah Winn declared their intentions to marry. On 18/3/1685 they continued their intentions of marriage and were given liberty to marry.

11/2/1685. Jacob Abrahams and Isabella Omealia declared their intentions to marry. [The m. 28/3/1685.]

11/2/1685. John Edmondson, Jr., and Susanah Omelia declared their intentions to marry. [They m. 28/3/1685.]

11/2/1685. George Furby signified that he had an intention to go to Pennsylvania and might reside there; requests a certificate.

18/3/1685. The estates of Thomas Taylor and Bryon Omealia were appraised.

18/3/1685. A difference has arisen betwixt John Wootters and John Keeld.

18/3/1685. It is reported that Stephen Durdon has brought a blemish upon truth and friends through his disorderly proceedings in taking a wife and other disorderly proceedings.

3/5/1685. Hannah Furby addressed the meeting by the advice of Ra. Fishburn and John Pemberton whom her dec'd. husband had left to advise her relating to his last will.

3/5/1685. Considering the age of William Fisk and his wife, he requests a meeting be kept at his house.

3/5/1685. The widow Mitchell desires Friends' advice relating to her dec'd. husband's concerns both locally and at Jones.

3/5/1685. Henry Parrott's last will was read in the meeting.

14/6/1685. It was proposed and approved that the meeting look after the children of Tho: Taylor, dec'd.

23/8/1685. Friends appointed to discourse with widow Willcocks concerning her proposal to the meeting of removing herself and son [apparently some place near Kings Creek].

23/8/1685. A dispute has arisen concerning the dividing part of Bryon Omelia's estate in as much as the widow Omealia and Bryon's two eldest daus. are removed by death before the debts and legacies were paid. Mary Omealia's will being disputed concerning her disposing of son to Wm. Sharp and did afterward leave him verbally to her brother and sister, Ralph and Sarah Fishbourn.

11/1/1686. William Kenton and Mary Parrott declared their intentions to marry. [William Kenton of Lankepor [Lancaster] Co. and Mary Parrattt, relique of Henry Parratt m. 13/2/1687.]

11/1/1686. It is the sense of this meeting that it was the intent of Bryon Omealia upon his death bed that his land at Appaquinimie should be sold for Negroes.

14/11/1686. This meeting understands that Ra: Fishbourn intends to put Bryon Omealy's two daus. abroad to school which this meeting with the women's meetings has thoroughly weighed and considered and it is their sense that the eldest daughter is in her place at present unless any misusage which this meeting does not fear and as to the youngest it is both the men and women's sense that she is too young to go out to school.

23/2/1686. Quarterly. Lovelace Gorsuch says he has been unable to attend meetings because of his wife's sickness.

7/3/1686. Tho: Adkisson produced a certificate from the meeting he belonged to in England and another from the magistrates and church wardens so called.

7/3/1686. Wm. Kennerly produced a certificate from the meeting he belonged to in England.

7/3/1686. Tho: Everndon delivered the will of George Johnson.

2/5/1686. The concern of Anne Spooner [widow of John] relating to her husband's will was referred to the next Quarterly Meeting.

27/6/1686. Ralph Fishbourn informed the meeting that there is 400 a. of land sold on bargaine made for in the territories of PA belonging to Bryant Omealia's estate by reason of which there is damage done to the sd. land. This meeting advises the execs. of Bryon Omealia to put a speedy stop to the sale so there may be no more damage done to sd. land.

**2/5/1686. Abraham Morgan and Eliza: Jenkinson declared their intentions to marry. On 30/5/1696 they announced their intentions for a second time and were given liberty to come together in marriage.

27/6/1686. Tho: Hutchinson informed this meeting he sold some land in West Jersey to James Harrisson upon several conditions whereof none was performed; the matter will be debated with the orphans of James Harrisson and their mother represented.

27/6/1686. Nathaniel Cleeve proposes to remove to PA.

24/7/1686. William Worrilow's paper of condemnation was presented.

22/8/1686. James Ridley and Rebeccah Berry declared their intentions to marry. [They m. 28/9/1686 at Kings Creek Meeting House.]

16/10/1687. A visit to Richard Mitchell finds that he does not regard the Love of God in Friends.

16/10/1687. William Stevens and Jane Atkinson declared their intentions to marry. [William Stevens of Transquaking in Dorchester Co. and Jane Atkinson, relique of Thomas Atkinson, m. 15/12/1687.]

10/12/1687. Edward Clarke is lately come into this province.

10/12/1687. A visit to Robert Register who is one of those lately come into this Province to dwell reveals his need for provisions which the meeting took care of.

24/12/1687 (Quarterly meeting). Estate of Tho: Adkinson was appraised. The woman has given to her three children 6 shillings each more than their part.

1/5/1687. Friends have visited John and Naomi Dixon amd discussed their daughter.

21/8/1687. Concern for orphans of Tho: Taylor.

21/8/1687. Concern for the widow Billeter.

14/10/1688. George Bowse's paper of condemnation for forward speaking in favour of wrong spirits was read.

29/4/1688. Joseph Rogers signified he was inclined to marry Thomas Booker's daughter; he was advised to refrain her company for the present. On 11/11/1688 Joseph Rogers and Mary Booker declared their intentions to marry.
[They m. 10/12/1688.]

6/2/1688. A box of hatts has arrived from England consigned to Bryon Omealia, dec'd.

6/2/1688. Wm. Troth and Isabella his wife proposed to this meeting the selling of land in England that belongs to Isabeall his wife, desiring the advice of Friends; much of the money would benefit James Harrison's orphans.

6/2/1688. Thomas Cooke complained that Samuel Wosley has left the plantation and mill which said Cook bought of James Peacock, much out of repair contrary to bonded agreement.

6/2/1688. Inspection of Tho: Taylor's plantation reveals that the orchard is much dimnified and the plantation much out of repair.

27/5/1688. The Meeting encourages John Dickenson's good resolution in not giving his consent to his daughter's marrying contrary to Truth; it is found that his wife is not one with him.

19/8/1688. Concern for the orphan children of Nathaniel Cleeves.

2/9/1688 (Quarterly meeting). Thomas Taylor was advised to go home with his uncle Jno. Pitt and Aunt until he is otherwised disposed of and that he keep to meetings with his uncle.

7/12/1689. Thomas Rennells and Anne Register declared their intentions to marry. [They m. 13/1/1690.]

4/2/1689. Some accompt [account] indicates that widow Milson is either married or intends to marry very speedily; an effort will be made to secure the children's estate according to their father's will.

**26/5/1689. Mosses Price and Dorrothy Rogers declared their intentions to marry. On 28/8/1689 they announced their intentions for the second time and were given liberty to come together in marriage.

26/5/1689. Several differences have arisen betwixt Henry Wollchurch and John Edmondson so that they have both been in a passion and run into bad and unsavoury expressions.

26/5/1689. Samuel Wosly says he will be more diligent in keeping to meetings.

28/8/1689. Anne Beal has been visited several times and advised to refraine from the man's company and not to proceed to marriage which advice she rejected and is now married.

28/8/1689. Michaell Russell seems to be sorry and ashamed of his outgoings.

15/9/1689. James Kersey seems sorry and ashamed for his outrunnings.

15/9/1689. John Vickers being removed by death the meeting advises Tho. Cook and John Ashdell to make an inventory of his estate and an appraisement with the aid of John Wooters.

30/10/1690. The placing of Thomas and John Taylor is referred to next meeting.

30/10/1690. The last will of William Berry was read; his son Wm. Berry was advised to get the will approved and make an inventory of his father's estate and get the assistance of those Friends named in his father's will.

9/11/1690. Tho: Taylor will be placed with Peter Harwood until he arrives at the age of 21, to learn the trade of cooper and carpenter.

9/11/1690. The youngest son of widow Parrott will be placed out and she will be supplied with provisions for the present.

6/12/1690. Richard Ratcliff and Mary Catternan declared their intentions to marry; the meeting asks that Richard Ratcliff verify that he is clear from any entanglement with the daughter of Henry Baker of PA, a Quaker. [Richard Ratclift, lawyer of Talbot Co. and Mary Caterne, m. at Tuckahoe Meeting House, 13/3/1691.]

6/12/1690. George Goult and Mary Sockwell, Jr., declared their intentions to marry. [They m,. 6/3/1691.]

6/12/1690. To speak with widow Willcocks to know her mind concerning her son, whether she is willing he be bound apprentice.

3/2/1690. There is a difference likely to arise betwixt Thomas Cook, Wm. Inchboard and widow Parrott concerning the lines of some land.

2/3/1690. George Pratt and Mary Parrott declared their intentions to marry. [They m. 2/5/1690.]

2/3/1690. Ralph Fishbourn advised to make over the land mentioned in Bryon Omealia's will to the use of his daughter Mary Omealia.

24/4/1690 (Quarterly meeting). Ralph Fishbourn desires a place to put Bryon Omealia in that Fishbourne's wife is dead and he is much abroad and has none at home but servants.

27/4/1690. Wm. Winsloe being under dealing. At a subsequent meeting he submitted a letter of condemnation.

22/6/1690. Peter Harwood and Eliza. Taylor declared their intentions to marry. [They m. 20/7/1690.]

4/1/1691 A certificate was granted to William Dixon.

8/11/1691. James Berry and Elizabeth Pitt declared their intentions to marry. [They m. 11/12/1691.]

5/12/1691. William Worrilow and Margarett Pinner declared their intentions to marry. [They m. 6/1/1691.]

1/3/1691. Thomas Cook, a resident for some time, intends for England and desires a certificate.

25/4/1691. To inspect the welfare of John West's orphans and to take part of their estate which is in the hand of their mother-in-law, Jone West, until they come of age.

30/5/1691. Nathaniel Cleeve's orphans to stay with James Wilson until next meeting and they to be at the meeting.

16/8/1691. James Edmondson and Magdalen Stevens declared their intentions to marry. [They m. 18/10/1691.]

27/10/1692. Anne Jadwin, widow, desires the meeting to advise her on matters relating to her dec'd. husband's estate.

6/11/1692. Jacob Bradbury and Anne Jadwin declared their intentions to marry. [They m. 19/12/1692.]

6/11/1692. William Edmondson and Sarah Sharp declared their intentions to marry. [They m. 25/12/1692.]

6/11/1692. Ann Jadwin [widow of Bartholomew Jadwin] will give her third part of all the plate of her dec'd. husband to her son Jeremiah Jadwin, to be delivered when he comes of age.

5/12/1692. William Dixon informs the meeting that his daughter-in-law has married by a priest in the night contrary to the wishes of himself and his wife.

5/12/1692. A difference has arisen between Henry Woolchurch and John Edmondson.

29/2/1692. Elias Goddard and Jone West declared their intentions to marry. They m. 29/3/1692.]

22/5/1692. Jeophrey Hardman and Elizabeth Booker declared their intentions to

marry. [They m. 21/6/1692.]

19/6/1692. John Dickenson and Rebecca Thomas declared their intentions to marry. [They m. 23/7/1692.]

19/6/1692. Obadiah Judkin, Jr., and Elizabeth Parrott declared their intentions to marry. [They m. 22/7/1692.]

16/7/1692. George Pratt and Elizabeth Parrott, Sr., declared their intentions to marry. [George Pratt and Elizabeth Parratt, relique of George Parratt m. 19/8/1692.]

16/7/1692. Kenelm Skillington and Lidiah Croxton declared their intentions to marry. [Kenellam Skillington and Lydia Croxtill, late of Barbadoes, m. 20/8/1692.]

26/10/1693. William Kenton removed by death. The meeting enquires into what care he took for his sons and also his son-in-law.

8/10/1693. John Edmondson has runn into several unsavoury and hard words against Samuell Jennings, alledging Samuel Jennings had wronged him, but the meetings does not agree.

23/4/1693. William Kenton intends to remove to Salem [with his wife to live] if Friends have nothing against it.

10/9/1693. Benjamin Parrott is asked to be at the next meeting to discuss the disrepair of Henry Parrott's plantation on which Benjamin Parrott lives.

10/9/1693. Informed that Nathaniel Cleeve's son lives with John Ashdell and has not had the schooling as directed by his father's will.

10/9/1693. Jon. Wilkinson, a Friend and cousin to Jno. Vickers, dec'd., has administered the estate of said Vickers, being largely in debt.

10/9/1693. Thomas Berry chooses as his guardian, James Ridly, provided he gives him a year's schooling and afterwards to go to a trade; Naomie Berry to have benefit of the plantation for the ensuing year and ½ of the profit of the orchard.

**2/1/1694. Ralph Elston and Mary Ball declared their intentions to marry. At the next meeting they announced their intentions a second time [... too faint to read.]

7/10/1694. Sarah Edmondson appeared in brokeness of heart and spirit and declared that whereas she had lett a spirit of straitness enter her against some

Friends in so much as she refused to give them her hand.

18/5/1694. William Kennerly's house has burned, losing all that was in it. A total of £5.2.6 was collected for his relief.

17/6/1694. The daus. of Bryon Omealia and John Dawson who is one of their husbands being at the meeting and each declaring that they had not done well in doeing as they had done in proceeding in marriage against the mind of Friends.

17/6/1694. Daniell Poweel [Powell] and Susanah Pitt declared their intentions to marry. [They m. 20/7/1694.]

16/6/1695. David Arey and Hannah Jadwyn, Jr., declared their intentions to marry. On 20/10/1695 David Arey and Hannah Jadwin declared their intentions to marry a second time. [They m. 1/11/1695.]

20/10/1695. Kenelm Skillington and his wife have neglected attending meetings.

30/11/1695. William Stevens, Jr., and Eliza: Edmondson declared their intentions to marry. [They m. 5/12/1695.]

31/8/1695. The care of Isaiah Parrott was before the meeting which desires his uncle Benja: Parrott to be at the next monthly meeting.

16/6/1695. Wm. Kennerly and John Foster to get the meeting houses in Dorchester Co. put upon record at their next county court; likewise James Ridly and James Berry will do the same for Talbot Co.

30/11/1695. A paper of condemnation submitted by George Bows was read.

26/2/1695. Thomas Berry with advice of his relations and Friends of Tuccahoe, intends to bind himself to his bro. James Berry to learn to be a boatwright, for 3 years.

24/3/1695. John Stacy and Martha Sockwell declared their intentions to marry. [They m. 5/5/1695.]

16/6/1695. Concern for Solomon West, son and orphant of John and Jone West.

12/7/1695. The meeting was advised of the disorderly living of Tho: Allcock and his wife.

12/7/1695. Stephen Dordon offered a paper of condemnation.

31/8/1695. The meeting thinks it convenient that Solomon West, orphant of John and Jone West, live with his father-in-law, Elias Goddard until his grandfather sends a special order for him or that Friends see cause to remove him.

28/9/1695. Stephen Dordon and Rebeccah Anderson declared their intentions to marry. [Stephen Durdan and Rebechah Anderson, relique of Thomas Anderson m. 1/11/1695.]

28/11/1696. This meeting advises all Friends that take any orphants either left by their parents or otherwise that they make use of the first opportunity of having them bound at the Court.

25/12/1696. Informed that Dorchester Co. Court has bound Solomon West to Matthias Allford.

25/12/1696. Alice Kennerly, widow of Wm. Kennerly, dec'd., desired tis meeting's advice on proceeding in regard to her husband's estate. She promised to divide the estate amongst her children properly. Joseph Kennerly, eldest son of Wm. Kennerly promised not to take advantage of his eldership upon his younger brother.

25/12/1696. This meeting reviewed a paper from Cecil Weekly Meeting signifying Stephen Coleman and Sarah his wife have a desire to remove to Pennsylvania.

25/4/1696. Lovlace Gorsuch and Hannah Wally declared their intentions to marry. [They m. 11/6/1696.]

27/6/1696. Rebeccah Dordon's paper of condemnation was read.

27/6/1696. Informed of John Nunam's disorderly practices and that he has contrary to the good order of Truth taken a wife by a priest and not above ten days after the buriall of his last wife.

29/8/1696. Charles Lewis appeared and declared that he and his wife had been often grieved that they were married by a priest.

26/9/1696. Thomas Booker and Eleanor Orem declared their intentions to marry. [They m. 3/11/1696.]

30/10/1697. Henry Parrott and Sarah Taylor declared their intentions to marry. [They m. 3/12/1697.]

30/10/1697. Thomas Buckingham and Katherine Parrott declared their intentions to marry. [Thomas Buckingham of Kent Co. and Catharine Parratt m. 3/12/1697 at Tuckahoe Meeting House.]

24/12/1697. Benjamin Parrott and Elizabeth Ashdell declared their intentions to marry. [Benjamin Parratt and Elizbeth Estell, both of Talbot Co., m. 6/2/1698 at Tuckahoe Meeting House.]

24/12/1697. John Pitt has an inclination to remove himself and wife to PA.

1/5/1697. Elizabeth Taylor condemns her action of being married by a priest.

1/5/1697. John Forder who lives upon the plantation of Nathaniell Cleeve, dec'd., complains that the rent is too high.

1/5/1697. William Harrison desired the meeting to advise him how to proceed in relation to his brother James Harrison's estate. The meeting advised him not to take advantage nor to deprive his bro. nor sister of what belongs to them.

31/1/1698. The following persons are to record births and burials:
Tredhaven Meeting: Abrah. Morgan
Choptanck Meeting: Danl. Powell
Tuccahoe Meeting: John Baynard
Bayside Meeting: Wm. Fishbourn
Transquaking Meeting: Joseph Kennerly
Chester Meeting: Edwd. Frey
Cecill Meeting: Ed. Beck.

1/10/1698. Wm. Fishbourn, about to remove to Philadelphia, requests a certificate.

1/10/1698. Robert Register and Mary Booker declared their intentions to marry. [Robert Rechester and Mary Booker, relique of Thomas Booker, both of Talbot Co., m. 1/11/1698 at Third Haven Meeting House.]

29/10/1698. Reports of John Grayson's untruthlike behaviour.

26/11/1698. Jane Judkin, widow to Obadiah Judkin, complained that she had been hardly dealt with by Wm. Sharp, exec. of her dec'd. husband and Tho. Taylor who had the tuition of Obadiah's granddaughter who is heir to his estate, others having said likewise, that she was hardly dealt by.

26/11/1698. John Grayson acknowledged he had drank too much.

23/12/1698. William Harrison and Eliza: Dickenson declared their intentions to marry. [They m. 20/2/1699.]

23/12/1698. William Treco acquainted the meeting that he had a servant taken away by execution (for the 40 lbs. of tobacco per poll to the priest).

23/12/1698. Joseph Atkinson and Naomie Wright declared their intentions to marry. [They m. 2/2/1699.]

**23/12/1698. Joseph Thompson and Eliza: Dawson declared their intentions to marry. They appeared at the next meeting and announced their intentions a second time and were given liberty to marry.

28/5/1698 (Quarterly meeting). Jonathan Ary requests a certificate.

1/7/1698. Howell Powell, Jr., and Joanna Prior declared their intentions to marry. [They m. 6/8/1698.]

1/7/1698. Richard Sutton of Philadelphia and Mary Howell of Cecill Co. declared their intentions to marry. He produced a certificate from the monthly meeting in Philadelphia, and because of the great distances involved asked permission to make their second announcement at the Cecil Monthly Meeting which was approved.

1/7/1698. Richard Dawson and Susanah Forster of Dorchester Co. declared their intentions to marry. [They m. 23/8/1698.]

28/7/1698. George Bowes finds drawings in his mind to remove himself and wife into old England to dwell.

28/7/1698. James Woolford and Grace Stevens declared their intentions to marry. [They m. 3/9/1698.]

**30/1/1699. Thomas Berry and Sarah Goddard declared their intentions to marry. At the next meeting the announced their intentions the second time and were given liberty to come together in marriage.

28/10/1699. Robert Jadwyn and Martha Wootters declared their intentions to marry. [They m. 11/12/1699.]

28/10/1699. There is a difference betwixt Kennelmn Skillington and Wm. Edmondson.

28/10/1699. A difference exists between Lovelace Gorsuch, Dorrothy Stevens and her son.

27/2/1699 (Quarterly meeting). The meeting is concerned for William Worrilow and his wife Margarett who in their unwatchfullness suffered the enemie of their soul peace ... discord that they parted each from the other and the woman left her husband and habitation near five weeks space; she has promised amendment but the man has not condescended as much as Friends could desire.

29/4/1699. Richard Mitchell addressed the meeting desiring that the meeting would please to order the administrators of his dec'd. father to render him an accompt of his estate in the Territory of PA.

29/4/1699. Richard Hall and Jane Judkins declared their intentions to marry. [Richard Hall and Jane Judkins, relique of Obadiah Judkins, m. 6/1699.]

29/4/1699. Thomas Edmondson and Mary Grason declared their intentions to marry. [Thomas Edmondson and Mary Grasum, relique of Robert Grasum, both of Talbot co., m. 7/6/1699 at Third Haven Meeting House.]

31/6/1699. James Taylor and Isabella Atkinson declared their intentions to marry. [They m. 1/8/1699.]

31/6/1699. Edward Fisher and Frances Willis declared their intentions to marry. [Edward Fisher of Dorchester Co., and Frances Willis, relique of Richard Willis of Dorchester Co., m. 1/8/1699 at Tuckahoe Meeting House.]

28/7/1699. It was reported that John Grayson has sworn several oaths and has been seen to be drunk at our last County Court and to speak bad language and vanity to swear.

30/9/1699. The meeting is concerned for the preservation of Eleannour Rigby alias Orem and the roads being so bad that is is hard for women to get to her house; therefor two men are to visit her.

28/1/1700. Elizabeth Sharp brought the will of Obadiah Judkins saying that her husband was removed by death who was the exec. of sd. Judkins and the meeting appointed Richd. Hall who m. the relict of said Judkins to be exec. in Wm. Sharp's place.

28/1/1700. John Willson and Frances Woosley declared their intentions to marry. [John Wilson and Frances Worsley of Talbot Co., m. 28/2/1700 at Tuckahoe Meeting House.]

28/1/1700. Richard Webb and Rebeccah Parrott declared their intentions to marry. [They m. 1/3/1700.]

28/1/1700. George Pratt and Sarah Broadaway declared their intentions to marry. [They m. 12/3/1700.]

26/10/1700. William Worrilow and Sarah Mackee declared their intentions to marry. [They m. 10/12/1700.]

26/10/1700. John Lowe and Mary Barclett, Jr. declared their intentions to marry. [John Lowe and Mary Bartlett m. 2/12/1700 at Third Haven Meeting House.]

26/10/1700. William Register and Sarah Booker declared their intentions to marry. [They m. 2/12/1700.]

26/10/1700. William Stevens, Jr., and Mary Prior declared their intentions to marry. [They m. 6/12/1700.]

25/2/1700. A certificate for John Pemberton, he intending to go to England.

31/5/1700. John Mitchell has taken a wife by a priest contrary to discipline.

26/7/1700. George Palmer complained that Wm. Dixon formerly sold him some land and that John Edmondson in his lifetime got a judgment against sd. Palmer for sd. land and by virtue of said judgment his sons vizt., James and Wm. Edmondson, claim sd. land and demand 3 year's rent.

31/10/1701. Richard Cribb and Anne Ashdell declared their intentions to marry. [Richard Cribb and Anne Estell, both of Talbot Co., m. 11/12/1701 at Tuckahoe Meeting House.]

28/11/1701. John Wootters, Sr. [of Tuccahoe Meeting], being removed by death, his eldest son endeavours to damn his will which if he does, it will be a great loss to the younger children.

25/12/1701. From Bayside Meeting: Robert Kemp has a daughter who ran away with a man to be married.

25/12/1701. Thomas Tiler and Eliza. Dean declared their intentions to marry. [Thomas Tyler and Elizabeth Dane, both of Talbot Co., m. 3/3/1702 at Choptank Meeting House.]

1/3/1701. In as much as Friend Wm. Stevens is removed by death who was appointed in Choptanck Meeting for visiting families, Howell Poweel, Jr. is appointed in his stead.

29/3/1701. Reported that somethng disorderly has happened between Robert Register and his wife.

29/3/1701. Thomas Taylor and Eliza. Sharp declared their intentions to marry. [They m. 21/6/1701.]

31/5/1701. Eliza. Taylor, relict of the exec. of Obadiah Judkin desires this meeting to take over the administration and Richard having married Obadiah Judkins widow this meeting desires John Baynard and John Wootters to speak to him to be at next meeting.

31/5/1701. Margarett Lecompt condemns herself and that spirit that drew her into that gross evil of running to the priest for a husband and marrying a man that made no profession of the blessed truth.

31/5/1701. Christopher Pennock being suddenly removed by death; an inquiry will be made into the account of his estate.

31/5/1701. The meeting is informed that John Toas has taken letters of administration upon the estate of Sutton Quinny, dec'd., whose widow Toes married who since is dead.

28/6/1701. Jeremiah Jadwyn and Isabella Harrison declared their intentions to marry. [They m. 9/9/1701.]

28/6/1701. The meeting chose Tho: Taylor of Kings Creek to be exec. of Obadiah Judkins.

28/6/1701. James Ridly intends to remove with his family to Salem in West Jersey.

29/9/1701. Informed that Willm. Edmondson has taken the oaths customary for magistrates and accepted the position of magistrate.

29/9/1701. William Troth states he bought a parcel of land of Joseph Rogers which is taken away by an elder survey and Joseph Rogers refuses to reimburse him unless he recovers it by law.

26/1/1702. Wm. Dixon informs the meeting that he has taken out a provincial writ against James Edmondson notwithstanding which he says he will desist if he may have his debt, and is willing to refer the matter to Friends.

26/1/1702. From Bayside Meeting - As to Robert Kemp's daughter, she is not yet married and care is taken to advise several priests not to do it and John Lillingston has sent a letter to Robt. Kemp to let him know that he will not do it without his consent but advises him to let them marry rather than live in incontinency.

30/10/1702. John Pitt complains that Robert Register owes him a debt and takes no care to pay it.

30/10/1702. Elizabeth Berry has run out from Truth and gone to the priest and is married to Jno. Sherwood.

30/2/1702 (Quarterly meeting). John Booker having been executed for the 40 per poll to the priest and the sheriff having got tobacco from him and he having no particular account, he is advised to go to the high sheriff for a particular accompt.

24/4/1702. John Lawrence and Martha Millson declared their intentions to marry - he is advised to get a certificate from the monthly meeting he belongs to in Pennsylvania if possible but at least from his father. [John Lawrence and Martha Wilson, both of Talbot Co. m. 9/7/1702 at Tuckahoe Meeting House.]

24/4/1702. The meeting understands that Walter Trotter has dealt with the sheriff and taken [bought] tobacco that was executed for the priest hire and several reports concerning his deportment.

24/4/1702. William Troth and Joseph Rogers are at law about some land.

27/6/1702. John Edmondson is removed by death; nothing has been done concerning the debt due to Wm. Dixon.

29/8/1702. The certificate returned by James Ridly is a false copy; the meeting ordered some lines to be writt to some honest Friend in Salem to communicate to the monthly or quarterly meeting to manifest James Ridly's untruth.

29/8/1702. A certificate received for Richard Walters from Philadelphia, dated 2/3/1702.

26/9/1702. The last will of Alice Kennerly was read wherein she willed her Negro woman Betty and her child to Dan Cox in consideration that he should pay 20 shillings annually for the full term of 30 years to this meeting for the paying of travelling[?] Friend's ferriage in Dorchester Co.

29/10/1703. Joseph Rogers is gone from the truth and is married to a wife by a priest.

29/10/1703. William Tippens having run out from truth and is married by a priest to Richard Hall's daughter

26/11/1703. Tuccaho Meeting reports that widow Pemberton went to a magistrate and is married to Robert Grundy, notwithstanding Friends labor.

26/11/1703. From Tuccaho meeting: The matter relating to George Bows and his --- is before this meeting.

24/12/1703. Peter Sharp and Katherine Troth declared their intentions to marry. [They m. 4/3/1704.]

24/12/1703. Edward Leeds and Ruth Ball declared their intentions to marry. On 30/1/1704 they announced their intentions the second time and were given liberty to accomplish their intentions.

24/12/1703. Howell Powell and Hester Bartlett declared their intentions to marry. [They m. 2/2/1702.]

24/12/1703. Howell Poweel [Powell] said that he and Robert Grundy had a difference and with provocation he struck him for which he is sorry.

24/12/1703. William Thompson and Mary Hall declared their intentions to marry. [They m. 4/2/1704.]

24/12/1703. Thomas Baynard and Hester Pratt declared their intentions to marry. [Thomas Baynard and Esther Pratt m. 19/2/1704 at Tuckahoe Meeting House.]

1/2/1703. There is a matter of difference betwixt John Jadwyn and William Sharp about a parcel of land called Chesnutt Bay[?] which was bequeathed by Peter Sharp in his last will to Jno. Garey and by Jno. Garey sold to John Jadwin which sd. land Wm. Sharp who was grandchild to the afsd. Peter Sharp claimed as heir at law notwithstanding the afsd. sale and bequest, whereupon they agreed to said difference to arbitration which was decided adversely to Wm. Sharp.

29/2/1703 (Quarterly meeting). Ralph Fishbourn requested a certificate, he not yet having had any since his removal to Pennsylvania.

27/3/1703. John Wooters in his last will desired that his estate might be divided and had appointed 4 Friends to divide the same; his eldest sons Richard and John Wootters were present at the meeting and requested advice.

27/3/1703. John Lawrence and his wife Martha submitted their papers of condemnation.

1/5/1703. James Kirkham and Affrica Dordon declared their intentions to marry; James is ordered to bring from under his mother and sister's hands to certify his clearness from women and also a certificate from his meeting in Pennsylvania. [They m. 11/6/1703.]

1/5/1703. Jane Cloathier, daughter of Robert Kemp, condemns her being married by a priest to a man not of the Society.

1/5/1703. Elizabeth Collinson, daughter of Robert Kemp, condemned her being married by a priest to a man out of the Society.

1/5/1703. Elizabeth Sherwood was advised to go to the priest by which she was married and condemn her action publicly.

29/7/1703. The concern of Mathew Fearn's orphants is finished.

31/11/1704. From Bayside: She that was the widow and relict of Robert Clark is lately married to a man not of the Society; Ennion Williams was left exec. with her in her dec'd. husband's will.

31/3/1704. Peter Webb and Sarah Stevens, Jr., declared their intentions to marry. [They m. 5/5/1704.]

31/3/1704. Benjamin Parrott and Jane Clark, Jr., declared their intentions to marry. [They m. 9/5/1704.]

29/4/1704. William Fowkes and Mary Forster declared their intentions to marry. [William Foulks of Acamack in VA, and Mary Foster, Jr., of Dorchester Co., m. 2/6/1704.]

29/4/1704. William Ewbank and Hannah Hall declared their intentions to marry. [They m. 9/6/1704.]

27/5/1704 (Quarterly Meeting). From Chester Meeting. Morgan Brown was removed by death.

27/5/1704 (Quarterly meeting). From Cecil Meeting: George Warner was removed by death.

30/6/1704. Nicholas Lowe was left joynt exec. with Sarah Edmondson of the last will of William Edmondson of Dorchester Co. and guardianship of his children was left to his wife Sarah Edmondson but she was also removed by death with her husband. Peter Sharp who was uncle to the children desired to have responsibility of their tuition but the court refused unless he gave bond which he refused.

30/6/1704. Sarah Worrilow has turn her back upon the truth and Friends by going to a priest to be married.

27/7/1704. Emanuell Jenkinson and Elizabeth Jadwyn declared their intentions to marry. [They m. 1/9/1704.]

26/8/1704. Sarah Pitt who was keeper of the books and papers of the women's meeting was removed by death.

30/9/1704. The meeting concerned for the welfare of Rebeccah Berry advises her uncles in law Stephen Dordon and John Baker with Wm. Troth, Wm. Harrison, Daniel Powell and John Pitt are impowered to sell and let [rent] her plantation and receive her estate.

30/9/1704. William Parrott and Susanah Silvester declared their intentions to marry. [They m. 10/11/1704.]

30/9/1704. William Troth and Sarah Pratt declared their intentions to marry. On 30/10/1804 they were advised to make provisions for her children. [They m. 11/11/1704.]

30/9/1704. Robert Register and Sarah Neale declared their intentions to marry. [They m. 4/11/1704.]

26/10/1705. As requested William Tippin has gone to Priest Lillingston by whom he was formerly married and did condemn himself and the spirit by which he acted.

26/10/1705. John Bartlett requested a certificate of his behaviour and his clearness from women.

31/11/1705. Thomas Pratt, orphant of George Pratt was removed to his uncle Thomas Baynard.

31/11/1705. A young woman has laid a child to John Leeds and has taken an oath that it is his child which he neither confesses nor denies.

26/2/1705. John Pitt and Daniel Poweel [Powell] who are the relations of James Berry's orphants were appointed to enquire of the father-in-law of sd. orphants how things stand in relation to their estate.

26/2/1705 (Quarterly meeting). From Transquaking meeting: To visit John Haines' daughter who it was said was like to be married by a priest.

28/4/1705. Naomie Berry intends to travel into parts of Pennsylvania and the Jerseys.

28/4/1705. Jonathan Taylor, son of Thos. Taylor, his certificate from the monthly meeting at Abbey Holme in Cumberland in old England was read.

26/5/1705 (Quarterly meeting). Abrah. Morgan appears for Tuccaho in Jno. Baynard's stead who is dead.

8/8/1705 (Quarterly meeting). Concern over placing George Pratt's orphant; his father and mother in law, viz. Wm. Troth and his wife to be at our next meeting.

8/8/1705 (Quarterly meeting). Roger Bradburry condemns his taking a wife out of the Truth and to go to a priest to be married.

29/9/1705. John Kemp and Mary Ball declared their intentions to marry. [They m. 1/11/1705.]

29/9/1705. The concern of the orphant of George Pratt being before this meeting and the meeting considering how and what condition he is in doe advise

Tho. Baynard who is married to sd. George Pratt's sister to goe to Samuel Broadaway and take the said orphant and carry him home to his aunt and keep him till next meeting and then bring him here but in case Saml. Broadaway should refuse to deliver him or the orphant refuses to goe with his uncle then this meeting advises Tho Baynard to apply himself to authority for the obteyning sd. orphant.

27/4/1706. Thomas Allcock and his wife's certificate was received from the monthly meeting to which they belonged in the county of Essex in England, dated 4/22/2704/5.

29/6/1706. John Pitt and Elizabeth Baynard declared their intentions to marry. [They m. 6/9/1706.]

31/10/1707. Phillip Morgan and Sarah Jadwyn declared their intentions to marry. [They m. 18/12/1707.]

27/11/1707 (Quarterly meeting). From Transquaking Meeting: An account that Jeremiah Jadwyn went to a priest and was by him sprinkled by the assistance of his mother and father in law, and his own wife contrary to Friends' order, interred a child of his in Friends burying ground and that also the aforenamed persons have neglected coming to meetings - therefore this meeting appoints George Bowes ... to visit them.

27/12/1707. Henry Clark and Sarah Parrott declared their intentions to marry. [They m. 21/2/1708.]

27/12/1707. Friends visited Jeremiah Jadwyn and Jacob Bradburry (who is his father in law).

**26/4/1707. John Ewbanck and Isabela Palmer declared their intentions to marry. They announced their intentions the second time and were given liberty to accomplished their intentions.

25/7/1707. David Arey and Elizabeth Cooke declared their intentions to marry. [They m. 12/9/1707.]

25/7/1707. Sarah Cape condemned her going to the priest for a husband.

27/11/1708 (Quarterly). Edward Clark acquainted the meeting that his son Henry Clark is removed to the western shore with a design to settle there and that he desires a certificate.

24/12/1708. William Dixon who was appointed to give account of the meeting is removed by death.

29/2/1708. William Leeds, a poor decreped man presented himself before the meeting pursuant to the advice of the last yearly meeting which was that he should be maintained by Friends provided he behaved himself orderly as becomes one professing Truth.

1/5/1708. From Treadhaven meeting: William Troth's wife is gone from him, there being a disagreement betwixt them.

1/5/1708. There being some difference between the trustees of John Jadwyn and Phillip Morgan who m. Sarah, daughter of sd. John Jadwyn, about the taking of inventory, the death of a Negro and the loss of some corn.

29/7/1708. Joseph Arey and Mary Baynard declared their intentions to marry. [They m. 10/9/1708.]

28/12/1709. Isaac Dixon and Elizabeth Harwood, Jr., declared their intentions to marry. They announced their intentions a second time and were given liberty to accomplish their intentions with advice of relations.

26/3/1709. John Stevens and Elizabeth Allcock declared their intentions to marry. [They m. 6/5/1709.]

26/3/1709. Abell Grace and Lidiah Ewbank declared their intentions to marry. [They m. 14/5/1709.]

31/6/1709. Robert Jones and Anne Lewis declared their intentions to marry. [They m. 24/9/1709.]

31/6/1709. Isaiah Parrott and Hannah Clark declared their intentions to marry. [Isaiah Pratt and Hannah Clark m. 9/9/1709 at Tuckahoe Meeting House.]

31/6/1709. Mary Swordin condemned her marrying by a priest.

29/7/1709. Stephen Durdon has brought a suit against John Pitt, administrator of the estate of John Stacy.

29/7/1709. William Dickenson informed that Emanuel Jenkenson has taken a horse from him by writ of replevin.

28/10/1710. George Bows has an inclination to put Anne Pratt to Philadelphia and desires the advice of the meeting.

31/11/1710 (Quarterly). An account was given by Ennion Williams in relation to the estate of George Warner that the persons chosen by Rebeccah Hosier and George Warner did meet and delivered to him his part of his father and mother's estate and also that part that was due to his sister Mary Warner and that the widow Hosier has a receipt from him for his part and also his bond to give security to the next county court for his sister's part which he has received.

29/4/1710. From Bayside: Benjamin Ball has married a wife contrary to Truth's order (who was one of the meeters belonging to that meeting).

29/4/1710. The meeting has received divers reports of the disorderly conversation of John Lawrence and that he has several times endeavoured to be married by a priest to Sarah Coughee.

29/4/1710. Daniel Maud of the City of London and Magdalen Stevens of Talbot Co. declared their intentions to marry; Daniel produced a certificate from the Two weeks Meeting in London dated 12/2/1708. [[They m. 17/6/1710.]

27/5/1710. Benjamin Ball has taken a wife contrary to Truth.

31/6/1710. John Lawrence disowned for taking a wife contrary to Truth.

28/7/1710. Transquaking Meeting: Elizabeth Haines has married by a priest to a person not in the Society

25/8/1710 (Quarterly meeting). Reference is made to Thomas Everndon, dec'd.

30/9/1710. Samuell Dickenson and Judith Troth declared their intentions to marry. [They m. 4/11/1710.]

30/9/1710. Thomas Adkinson and Rachell Judkin declared their intentions to marry. At the next meeting they announced their intentions a second time and were given liberty to accomplish their intentions.

28/1/1711. From Tuccaho Meeting: George Booker has appeared by way of testimony, he not having any certificate from Friends in old England from whence he came, having been sundry times advised to forbear publick preaching in our assemblys until he was properly recognized.

28/1/1711. At his request Ennion Williams was replaced by John Lowe to register births and burials.

28/1/1711. George Troth complained that the execs. of his father William Troth, dec'd., upon the division of the estate, took a bond from him the sd. George Troth in which bond he says there is a clause which he is dissatisfied with and has a difference betwixt him and said execs.

28/12/1711. Transquaking Meeting: Danll. Cox was removed by death.

25/2/1711. Thomas Taylor of Kingscreek, General Collector for the Quarterly Meeting, was removed by death.

30/3/1711. Magdalen Edmondson who once belonged to Tredhaven Meeting married contrary to Truth's order to a certain Jacob Loockerman; this meeting has in mind to visit her.

27/4/1711. George Troth has agreed with the execs. to allow them 6 1/2 per cent to his quarter part of his father's estate.

25/5/1711 (Quarterly meeting). Martha Baynard, now Martha Tillingston has married by a priest.

25/5/1711 (Quarterly). Cecil Monthly Meeting referred their further proceeding against Charity Spirman who has taken a husband contrary to Truth's order and run into divers other evil and light actions.

29/6/1711. Samuell John Ashdell, late of Talbot Co., who d. intestate, having a parcel of land in fee simple leaving two daus. who as coheirs enjoyed the said land but made no division thereof. Benja. Parrott m. the elder who is dead leaving John, a son. Richd. Cribb m. the younger who is yet living but not having issue.

29/6/1711. John Berry and Anne Pratt declared their intentions to marry. [They m. 10/8/1711.]

29/6/1711. Samuell Burberry complained that the trustees of John Jadwyn have not paid him the debt that John Jadwyn owed him. David Arey who is one of the said trustees is willing but the other trustee, Emanuell Jenkenson, is not.

26/7/1711. Eliza. King (who visited families of Bayside Meeting) is dead.

26/7/1711. Joseph Kennerly and Mary Stevens declared their intentions to marry. [They m. 14/9/1711.]

26/7/1711. James Bartlett intends to take a wife in Pennsylvania and requests a certificate.

26/7/1711. Of Choptank Meeting William Stevens and Eliza. Sharp (who visited families) have been removed by death and are replaced by Peter Webb and Rebeccah Dickenson.

26/1/1712. Thomas Cannor and Betey Cox declared their intentions to marry. [Thomas Cannon and Betty Cox, both of Dorchester Co., m. 14/3/1712 at Transquaking Meeting House.]

26/1/1712. Ennion William to remove to Pennsylvania (on a visit?).

28/3/1712. Nehemiah Beckwith and Francis Taylor declared their intentions to

marry. [They m. 10/5/1712.]

28/3/1712. Jno. Willis and Margrett Cox declared their intentions to marry. [They m. 10/5/1712.]

26/4/1712. Benjamin Ball condemned his taking a wife contrary to the way prescribed by the Truth.

28/6/1712. Whereas many great and disorderly differences have a long time continued between Philip Morgan and his wife [Sarah] notwithstanding care and labour at sundry times to reclaim them, they still persist in their difference to the great grief of this meeting.

**28/6/1712. Danll. Richardson and Ruth Leads declared their intentions to marry. Daniel produced a writing from under the hands of Samll. Gallaway and Mordic.. More which signified that care would be taken to send a certificate to next monthly meeting. Mary Ellston, mother of sd. Ruth Leads, signified by writing that she had given her consent. On 24/7/1712 they announced their intentions a second time and were given liberty to accomplish their intentions.

**27/9/1712. Edward Turnor and Lidia Durdin declared their intentions to marry. They declared their intentions a second time at the next meeting.

27/9/1712. There is a difference between Thos. Berry and Abraham Morgin.

24/11/1713. Eliza. Wooters condemns her disobeying her father and for taking a husband by a priest.

**30/7/1713. John Cooper and Daberah Smith declared their intentions to marry. They declared their intentions a second time at the next meeting and were given liberty to accomplish their intentions.

28/8/1713. Danll. Richardson and his wife Ruth condemned their disorderly walking.

28/2/1714 (Quarterly meeting). Benjamin Ball requested a certificate in regard to his clearness in marriage.

26/3/1714. In attempting to procure the dower right of the Mary Register from Robt. Bokers, to her late husband's land; the committee has been with Evin Pearse who m. the widow of Robert Boker; it was agreed that Evin Pearse should pay her the sum of 170 lbs. of tobacco yearly.

26/3/1714. Edward Turnor, Jr. and Lidia his wife condemned their untruth.

27/8/1714 (Quarterly meeting). Thomas Jadwin (son of Jno. Jadwin, late dec'd.), to be visited.

**24/9/1714. Wm. Baynard and Sasanah Pardo declared their intentions to marry. They appeared at the next meeting and announced their intentions a second time and were given liberty to accomplished their intentions.

29/10/1714. Friends who were appointed by last Yearly Meeting to inspect into the complaint of Jno. Pitt against George Warner report that they were with George Warner and Philip Reason who married the said Warner's sister but were unable to fully comply and defer to next Quarterly Meeting.

29/12/1715. Thomas Ball requests his tobacco for keeping Wm. Leeds.

28/5/1715. James Smith acquaints the meeting with his intention of leaving the Province and requests a certificate.

* 31/6/1715. Thomas Wilkison and Sarah Cox declared their intentions to marry. On 30/9/1715 it was reported that Thos. Willkinson's marriage was orderly accomplished.

28/7/1715. Stephen Dardain and Rebecca Hosher declared their intentions to marry. [Stephen Dorden of Talbot Co. and Rebechah, daughter of Henry Hosher late of Kent Co., dec'd., m. 2/9/1715 at Tuckahoe Meeting House.] On 30/9/1715 it was reported that Steven Dartain's marriage was accomplished at John Pitt's house; the people were something disorderly.

28/7/1715. Morgin Brown and Rebacka Dardin declared their intentions to marry; he is to bring a certificate from Cecil Monthly Meeting. [Morgan Brown of Kent co. and Rebechah Durden of Talbot Co., m. 7/10/1715 at Tuckahoe Meeting House.]

30/9/1715. From Tredhaven: Two widows, Ellenr. Booker and Eliza. Jenkinson, have gone from the truth and have taken husbands by the priest.

29/1/1716. Joshua Kenerly reports that Jno. Smith, weaver, stands justly indebted to him the sum of £3.15.

27/12/1716. Jeremiah Neall and <u>Ann</u> Lewes declared their intentions to marry. Jeremiah and Ann appeared at the next meeting and announced their intentions for a second time and were given liberty to marry. [Jeremiah Neal and <u>Elizabeth</u> Lewis, daughter of Charles Lewis, both of Talbot Co., m. 10/2/1717 at Tuckahoe Meeting House.]

30/3/1716. The meeting agreed with Judatus Harden to accommodate the widow Register from the 1st day of the 4th month next one year for which consideration he is to have the rent of her land this insuing year and Friends are to pay him the remaining part to make up the said rent the value of 1200 lbs. of tobacco in corne meal and at a reasonable price.

30/3/1716. From Tredhaven Meeting: Sarah Harwood has committed the sin of uncleanness.

30/3/1716. Susanah Berry has been joyned to a husband by a priest.

26/7/1716. James Willson, Jr., and Mary, daughter of Tho: Berry declared their intentions to marry. [They m. 19/10/1716.]

29/9/1716. Wm. Edmondson and Margrate, daughter of James Berry, dec'd., declared their intentions to marry. [They m. 3/11/1716.]

27/1/1717. David Farebanks has taken a wife by a priest.

25/10/1717. From Tuckaho Meeting: Widow Kent has gone to the priest and taken a husband.

30/11/1717. Rebecka some time wife of Wm. Kenton said she owned her transgression and was sorry.

26/12/1717. Samll. Neall and Hannah Webb declared their intentions to marry. [They m. 2/2/1718.]

29/3/1717. Thomas Hubanks, Jr. and Jane Clother declared their intentions to marry. [They m. 11/5/1717.]

29/3/1717. Wm. Kemp and Martha Hubanks declared their intentions to marry. [They m. 11/5/1717.]

27/4/1717. It was reported that Daniell and Howell Powell had sometime past been at Oxford and quarrelled and fought with some others.

31/5/1717 (Quarterly meeting). Peter Webb was removed by death.

25/7/1717. Samll. Dickenson requested a certificate to signify the clearness of his brother, James Dickenson, in relation to marriage.

27/9/1717. From Choptank Meeting: William Stevens was removed by death.

26/1/1718. Choptank Meeting: William Dickenson removed by death.

30/11/1718. Edward Clark, Sr., requested a certificate for Edward Clark, Jr., to signify his clearness in marriage.

25/12/1718. Tradhaven Meeting: Peter Harwood's daughter Mary was stolen away by one George Cumberford, she not being 16 years of age and were married by a priest [at Annapolis]. Peter Harwood is advised to engage with someone who is learned in the law.

25/4/1718. Thomas Taylor requested a certificate for John Taylor who is lately gone to England.

27/6/1718. Howell Powell and Sarah Edmondson declared their intentions to marry. [They m. 2/8/1718.]

27/6/1718. Howell Powell condemned his behavior.

24/7/1718. Tradhaven Meeting: Penelopy, daughter of Kenlin Skillington, notwithstanding being precautioned to the contrary, was married by a priest to a man out of the Society.

25/1/1719. To visit she who was widow Sarah Willkinson.

25/1/1719. William Mikell and Eliza. Errington declared their intentions to marry. [William Michael and Elizabeth Herrington, both of Talbot Co., m. 13/3/1719 at Tuckahoe Meeting House.]

*25/1/1719. John Berry and Tamer Willson declared their intentions to marry. On 27/3/1719 it was reported that the marriage of John Berry had been orderly accomplished.

27/11/1719. Difference between John Stevens and Edmondson Stevens concerning some land in joint tenancy.

27/11/1719. The reference from the monthly meeting in the 9th month last to this meeting that the meeting that used to be att the house of Sarah Stevens, dec'd., should be kept att Choptank Meeting being considered.

*27/3/1719. Samll. Harwood and Mary Dean declared their intentions to marry. On 24 4/1719 they announced their intentions a second time and were given liberty to marry. On 29/5/1719 it was reported that the marriage of Samll. Harwood and Mary Dean was effected in good order.

27/3/1719. Thomas Pott's certificate from Abington in Pennsylvania dated 27/2/1719 was received.

24/4/1719. Stephen Durdan and Mary Cox declared their intentions to marry. [They m. 19/6/1719.]

24/4/1719. From Tuckaho Meeting: Tho. Pratt was given to a priest and married to a wife.

***27/6/1719. William Harrison and Frances Powell declared their intentions to marry.

*30/7/1719. Wm. Ratlif and Mary Fellows declared their intentions to marry. John Ratliff and Sarah Fellows declared their intentions to marry. It was reported on 25/26th da., 9th mo., 1719 that the marriages of Jno. and Wm. Ratlift were accomplished in good order.

27/9/1719. Evan Jones appeared with a certificate from monthly meeting at Radnor in Pennsylvania, signifying his good conversation and clearness from women in relation to marriage.

31/1/1720. Jno. Parrat and Ruth Smith declared their intentions to marry. The above Jno. Parrat was removed by death before the monthly meeting in the 2nd month.

28/10/1720. Wm. Edmondson and Prislah Coall declared their intentions to marry. [William Edmondson of Dorchester Co. and Priscilla Cole m. 2/1/1720 at Choptank Meeting House.]

22/12/1720. James Smith requested a certificate of his clearness and unity.

22/12/1720. Calep Clark and Reba: Webb declared their intentions to marry. [They m. 2/5/1721 at Tuckaho Meeting House.]

28/2/1720 (Quarterly meeting). Richd. Webb being removed by death who was appointed to inspect the affairs of widows and orphans in Tuckaho Meeting.

25/3/1720. James Fucks [Fooks] and Elizabeth Kenerly declared their intentions to marry. [They m. 3/5/1720.]

27/5/1720 (Quarterly meeting). George Bows requested a certificate concerning his clearness in marriage; the certificate was directed to Kent Co., MD.

31/6/1720. Samll. Dickenson condemned his giving way to wrath and passion.

31/6/1720. Wm. Golt and Hannah Parrat declared their intentions to marry. [They m. 30/7/1720.]

*28/7/1720. Edmondson Stevens and Sidny Dickenson declared their intentions to marry. On 27/8/1720 they declared their intentions for the second time and were given liberty to accomplish their intentions. At the next meeting 30/9/1720 or 19/10/1720 it was reported that the marriage was performed in good order.

30/9/1720. James Ratliff and Sarah Warnor declared their intentions to marry. [They m. 12/11/1720.]

28/1/1721. The meeting understands that Elizabeth, daughter of John Berry, is willing to go to live with her uncle, Tho: Pratt and this meeting assents to it.

?/2/1721. James Willson, Jr. was appointed in the stead of Friend George Bows, dec'd.

1/12/1721. Sarah Cape, a poor decreped widow Friend, desires that Friends take her estate that she may be maintained.

27/5/1721. Even Jones, Doct., received a certificate to Pennsylvania from whence he came about two years earlier and now is returning, signifying a good opinion and his practice and also of his clearness in marriage.

30/6/1721. Tuckaho Meeting: There is a difference between Edward Clark and James Willson which Friends are unable to reconcile.

27/7/1721. James Retlif condemns his untruth action with her that is now his wife.

27/7/1721. Wm. Harrison and Eliza: Richardson declared their intentions to marry. [They m. 30/8/1721 at Bayside Meeting House.]

26/8/1721. Complaint was made that Thomas Hubanks, Jr., who m. the widow and relict of Robt. Clother, has abused some of the orphans of the sd. Robt. Clother at divers times.

*29/9/1721. Samll. Dunin and Tamer Berry declared their intentions to marry. On 1/12/1721 Samll. Duning's marriage was reported as accomplished in good order.

29/9/1721. Ennan Williams and Francis Bows declared their intentions to marry. [They m. 3/11/1721.]

26/10/1722. Peter Harwood and Grace Hopkins declared their intentions to marry. [They m. 14/12/1722.]

26/10/1722. Edward Parrish and Rachall Harwood declared their intentions to marry. [They m. 10/12/1722.]

31/11/1722. Edward Clark, Jr., has married by a Justice in Pennsylvania with the consent of his father.

31/11/1722. Transquaking Meeting: Joseph Kennerly was removed by death; replaced by Joshua Kennerly to record births and burials.

1/9/1722. Susannah Parratt [now Slater, Slaughter], widow of William Parratt, was married by a justice of the peace.

**31/11/1722. Jeremiah Jadwin [Jr.] and Eliza: Golt declared their intentions to marry [with consent of parents]. On 27-29/1/1723 they declared their intentions for a second time and were given liberty to marry.

31/11/1722. A certificate on the behalf of Margrat Bartlett from the monthly meeting at West River dated 4/11/1722 was received.

**31/11/1722. Joseph Willson and Rebacah Ridley declared their intentions to marry for the second time and were given liberty to marry.

31/11/1722. Peter Harwood and Thos. Atkinson produced a statement in this meeting under the hand of Rebacah Pitt, Rebackah Durdan and Ann Bradbery declaring it was their judgment that they believed that Ennion Williams's wife Francis did not go nine months with her late child and that they believed it was begot after marriage.

26/2/1722. From Bayside Meeting: Danll. Richardson and Tho: Ball removed by death.

*30-31/3/1722. Burtonwood Allcock and Johanan Stevens declared their intentions to marry. On 27-28 they declared their intentions for a second time and were left to their liberty to marry. On 26/4/1722 it was reported that the marriage was accomplished in good order.

27/4/1722. From Transquaking: Joshua Kennerly's daughter Martha was married by a priest.

26/5/1722. Peter Sharp complained that Thomas Bond, merchant in London, was justly indebted unto him; it had been the sense of this meeting Peter Sharpe should write to the sd. bond which he has done and has received no answer.

28/9/1722. James Smith's certificate signifying Friend unity with him dated at Salem, West Jersey Monthly Meeting the 17/6/1722.

27/1/1723. Concern for the orphan Thomas Kenerly, son of dec'd. Friend Joseph Kennerly of Dorchester Co.

30/11/1723. Whereas a difference has been for some time between Rebecca Dorden and Edward Turnor about paying his wife's portion. They have agreed that Rebecca Dorden is to give Edward Turnor one Negro boy named Jemey and one large copper kettle and one table and one feather bed to be paid on demand and also quitting all accounts that she has against the sd. Turnor and likewise promises that she will leave the said Turnor one mulatto girl named Dugony if the sd. girl be living at the decease of the sd. Rebecca.

26/12/1723. Abraham Morgan being removed by death.

23/2/1723. Thos. Kennerly orphan of Joseph Kennerly appeared with James Fucks [Fooks] his bro.-in-law and Mary Kenerly his sister with whose consent and agreement the sd. orphant is to be kept at school and boarded at Sarah Webb's at the charge of the rents arising from the real estate of the orphant.

**29/3/1723. Robt. Wallker and Mary Buckingham declared their intentions to marry. On 26/4/1723 they declared their intentions a second time and were given liberty to marry.

28/6/1723. Solomon Edmondson and Esther Kennerly declared their intentions to marry. [They m. 3/8/1723.]

28/6/1723. Edward Turnor reports that there is a difference between him and his mother-in-law Rebacah Durdan relating to the division of the estate of Steven Durdain, dec'd.

26/7/1723. Peter Sharp has a certificate from this meeting directed to Friends in Pennsylvania and the Jerseys signifying Friends unity.

*31/8/1723. Joshua Clark and Ann Parrat declared their intentions to marry. On 25/10/1723 the marriage of Joshua Clark was reported as well accomplished; there was some disorder.

25/1/1724. John Stevens of Talbot Co. was presented to Dorchester Co. Court as a person approved to be guardian to the orphan Thomas Kenerly but he was refused by the sd. court because he was not an inhabitant of Dorchester Co.

3/2/1724. John Dickenson and Rebekah Powell declared their intentions to marry. [They m. 11/4/1724.]

30/5/1724. Jno. Everett requested a certificate showing his clearness in marriage.

*26/6/1724. William Kennerly and Sarah Stevens declared their intentions to marry [a certificate was to be sent to Friends of Jersey]. The marriage was reported as orderly accomplished on 25/9/1724.

*30/7/1724. Aaron Parrat and Lidia Kenton declared their intentions to marry. On 12/9/1724 it was reported that the marriage had been orderly accomplished.

30/7/1724. James Berry and Sarah Skillington declared their intentions to marry. {They m. 12/9/1724.]

30/7/1724. Jonathan Taylor and Eliza: Sherwood declared their intentions to marry, with consent of parents. [They m. 12/9/1724.]

30/7/1724. Choptank Meeting: William Stevens who was a Friend's child, has gone and taken a wife out of the Truth and was married by a priest.

31/1/1725. Charles Dickenson and Sophia Richardson declared their intentions to marry. [They m. 8/5/1725.]

31/1/1725. Tuckaho Meeting: Brantwood [Burtonwood] Allcock and Jno. Cooper have gone to law.

31/1/1725. It was reported that Jno. Hubanks and Isabela his wife have both died and left two small children and that their grandfather, Thos. Hubanks, Sr., was willing they should be bound to John Ratliff to learn a trade with which the meeting has unity.

29/10/1725. Thos. Atkinson complained that Neomy Atkinson was indebted by 1690 lbs. of tobacco for which payment he has long waited.

27/11/1725. Danll. Cox and Ann Powell declared their intentions to marry. [They m.3/1/1725.]

23/12/1725. Neomy Atkinson complained of her inability to pay her bro.-in-law by reason of poverty; he was advised to use brotherly kindness and patience.

23/12/1725. Jno. Leeds and Rachall Harrison declared their intentions to marry [with consent of parents]. [They m. 14/2/1726.]

**26/3/1725. Joseph Arey and Jane Parrat declared their intentions to marry. On 30/4/1725 they declared their intentions a second time and were given liberty to marry.

26/3/1725. Wm. Stevens has gone to a priest declared their intentions to marry.

25/5/1725. Mary Golt has married out of the unity of Truth.

25/5/1725. John Wray desires a certificate [directed to London].

23/12/1725. George Willson requested the meeting to enquire into his conversation in relating to marriage in order to have a certificate [to be directed to Salsbery Monthly Meeting on Delaware].

26/6/1725. Henry Parratt condemned his marrying by a priest.

26/6/1725. It was reported that Eliza: Berry, orphan daughter of Jno. Berry was not being brought up among Friends.

29/7/1725. James Smith requested a certificate in relation to marriage [directed to Friends in Haddonfield, West Jersey].

29/7/1725. It was reported that the orphan Eliza: Berry is with her mother-in-law who is now wife of Samll. Dunnin [Dunning].

28/8/1725. Edward Neall and Eliza. Jones declared their intentions to marry. [They m. 1/10/1725.]

28/8/1725. John Farbanks, Jr., condemned his being married by a priest.

24/9/1725. Francis Neall and Ann his wife have produced a publick testimony declaring their sorrow for their transgressions.

**24/9/1725. Joseph Warnor and Ann Coll declared their intentions to marry. On 29-30/10/1725 they declared their intentions a second time and were given liberty to marry.

26/11/1726. Execs. of Levin Denwood appointed.

*22/12/1726. Curtiss Evans and Margarett Brannock declared their intentions to marry. On 27/2/1727 it was reported that the marriage of Curtis Evans and Margaret Brannock was orderly and decently performed.

22/12/1726. Sarah Webb desires payment for boarding the orphan Tho: Kennerly; the administrator will be spoken to.

29/4/1726. Tradhaven Meeting: Jno. Webb has gone out and been married by a priest to a woman not of the Society.

27/8/1726. Tho: Thompson requested a certificate of his clearness in marriage.

*30/9/1726. John Rawlings and Elizabeth Fooks declared their intentions to marry [with the consent of his mother and father]. On 26/11/1726 it was reported that the marriage of John Rawlings was accomplished in good order.

30/9/1726. A certificate was requested for John Edmondson with respect to marriage.

29/1/1727. James Wilson, Sr., on behalf of his son William Wilson, requested a certificate on his conversation and clearness in relation to marriage, to be directed to Salisburry Monthly Meeting.

27/10/1727. Kent Island Meeting: Benja.: Ball who was dangerously ill gave his report in writing.

28/12/1727. Transquaking Meeting: Mary Kennerly was m. by a priest.

**31/3/1727. William Taylor and Sarah Fookes declared their intentions to marry. On 28-29/4/1727 they declared their intentions a second time and were given liberty to marry.

***30/6/1727. James Talor and Rebeccah Buckingham declared their intentions to marry.

30/6/1727. From Tredhaven Meeting: Tho. Talor being removed by death.

26/8/1727. From Tredhaven Meeting: Howell Poweel [Powell] having through unwatchfulness was taken with strong drink for which he is sorry.

29/9/1727. From Bayside Meeting: Mary Low who was a Friend's daughter was m. by a priest.

28/1/1728. There is a difference between Samll. Dickenson and Sarah Weeb relating to lands in dispute.

30/11/1728. Informed that Isaiah Parratt, orphan of Isaiah Parratt, dec'd., is at his house according to the --- of the orphan's mother who is lately dead.

26/12/1728. It is the judgment of the meeting that Joshua Clark has a right to the guardianship of Isaiah Parrat.

25/2/1728. Wm. Sharp, son of Peter Sharp, plans to go to London and requests a certificate.

28/6/1728. Benja. Parrat and Debrough Arrey declared their intentions to marry. [They m. 27/7/1728.]

*31/10/1729. Wm. Scot and Jean Arey declared their intentions to marry. On 25/12/1729 it was reported that the marriage of Wm. Scot was decently accomplished.

29/11/1729. Jno. Dickenson and Eliza: Harrison, Jr., declared their intentions to marry. [The m. 29/3/1730.]

29/11/1729. Christopher Birkhead and Ann Harrison declared their intentions to marry. [They m. 1/1/1729.]

1/3/1729. A visit was made to Thos. Foster in regard to his being sprinkled and married by a priest; his mother says it was without her consent.

31/5/1729. Peter Sharp complains that Joshua Clark and Aaron Parrat possess some part of a tract of land of his called Johns Neck.

27/6/1729. Wm. Sharp and Ann Birkhead declared their intentions to marry. [They m. 23/8/1729.]

27/6/1729. Joseph George and Sarah Bartlett declared their intentions to marry, he producing a certificate from Kent Co., MD. [They m. 20/9/1729.]

27/6/1729. Tuckaho Meeting. It was reported that buried at Tuckaho graveyard was the wife of Thos. Silvester who was out of unity with Friends.

27/6/1729. James Powell and Hannah Parrat declared their intentions to marry. [they m. 21/8/1729.]

27/6/1729. Jane Thomas, sometime Hubanks, produced a paper in which she condemned her being married by a priest (who is now dead).

**28/9/1729. George Willson and Susanah Thrift declared their intentions to marry.

*25-26/1/1730. It was reported that the marriage of Christopher Birkhead's marriage was performed decently.

30/10/1730. Phillip Jenkins [Jenkinson] and Sarah Webb of Dover declared their intentions to marry. [They m. 4/12/1730.]

24/12/1730. Robart Harwood and Mary Darden [Durden] declared their intentions to marry. [They m. 13/2/1731.]

24/12/1730. Thomas Bartlet and Mary Regester declared their intentions to marry. [They m. 14/2/1731.]

30/2/1730. It was considered by the meeting that Jonathan Neall, orphan son of Samll. Neall, be under the care of his half-bro. John Webb who is to put him to school for one year and to maintain him and to have his plantation for the same time.

30/5/1730. Joshua Clark has m. by a priest.

30/5/1730. John Edmondson of Dorchester Co. and Mary Neall declared their intentions to marry. [They m. 3/7/1730.]

**26/6/1730. Isaac Cox and Sarah Turner declared their intentions to marry. On 30/7/1730 they declared their intentions of marriage a second time and were given liberty to marry.

30/7/1730. Edward Turnor requested a certificate in relation to marriage, to be directed to the monthly meeting in Kent Co., MD.

29/8/1730. Wm. Edmondson and Eliza: Troth, Jr. declared their intentions to marry [with consent of relations]. [They m. 1/10/1730.]

**29/8/1730. Stephen Thomas and Mary Clother declared their intentions to marry [with consent of parents]. On 30-31/10/1730 they declared their intentions a second time and were given liberty to marry.

29/8/1730. Henry Buckingham and Eliza: Low declared their intentions to marry. [They m. 3/10/1730.]

**29/8/1730. John Baynard and Eliza: Fisher declared their intentions to marry [with consent of parents].On 25-26/9/1730 they declared their intentions a second time and were given liberty to marry.

**29/10/1731. Park Webb and Grace Jones declared their intentions to marry. On 27/11/1731 they declared their intentions a second time and were given liberty to marry.

28/11/1731. Elizabeth Troth requested a certificate to Pennsylvania.

29/2/1731. Saml. Dickenson requests a certificate in regard to marriage [directed to Philadelphia].

*29/2/1731. William Richardson and Ann Webb declared their intentions to marry [with consent of parents]. On 30/4/1731 it was reported that the marriage of Wm. Richardson was performed in good order.

29/6/1731. Robert Clother requested a certificate in regard to his clearness in marriage, he having lived sometimes at the Bayside and sometimes with his mother.

*28/8/1731. Francis Regester and Margrett Bartlett declared their intentions to marry [with consent of parents]. On 29/10/1731 it was reported that the marriage of Francis Regtster had been decently accomplished.

28/8/1731. James Bartlett [son of Thos. Bartlett] and Sarah Hopkins declared their intentions to marry. [They m. 2/10/1731.]

*28/9/1731. John Walker and Mary Fooks declared their intentions to marry. On 28/12/1731 it was reported that the marriage of John Walker was accomplished in good order.

29/1/1732. Samuel Dickenson complains there is a difference between himself and Sarah Webb.

*28/4/1732. John Stevens and Elizabeth Troth declared their intentions to marry. On 30/6/1732 it was reported that the marriage of John Stevens was accomplished in good order.

27/5/1732. Edward Neel complained that there is some difference between himself and his bro. Francis about the right to some land.

27/5/1732. Robart Jadwin and his wife Mary condemned their marrying by a priest.

30/6/1732. George Willson requested a certificate in regard to his clearness in marriage [to be directed to the monthly meeting in Kent Co., DE].

28/1/1733. Wm. Sharp reported that there was some difference between himself and Elizabeth Stevens.

28/1/1733. Samuel Dickenson complained that there was a difference between himself and John Stevens.

27/12/1733. It was determined by a committee in the controversy of the will of Daniel Powell that the widow, Susannah, have one-third of the personal estate, and debts were paid.

27/12/1733. Isaac Cox and Rachel Skillington declared their intentions to marry. On 25/2/1734 it was reported that the marriage of Isaac Cox was accomplished in good order.

30/3/1733. Daniel Cox complained that there was a difference between himself and John Dickenson and the execs. of Daniel Powel.

30/3/1733. Fortune Lewes complained that Samuel Dickenson is in her debt for some part of the legacy given her by her grandfather, Wm. Troth, and refused to pay.

**27/5/1733. James Farebank and Elizabeth Neel declared their intentions to marry. On 29-30/6/1733 they declared their intentions a second time and were given liberty to marry.

**29/6/1733. Thomas Brannock and Frances Newton declared their intentions to marry. On 26-27/7/1733 they declared their intentions a second time and were given liberty to marry.

26/7/1733. Henry Thomas, son of Wm. Thomas of KE Co., MD, and Rebeckah Troth declared their intentions to marry. [They m. 9/9/1733.]

*8/9/1733. Samuel Bartlett, son of Thos. Bartlet and Rachel Turner declared their intentions to marry. On 28/10/1733 they declared their intentions a second time and were given liberty to marry. On 26-27/10/1733 it was reported that the marriage had been accomplished in good order.

8/9/1733. Francis Neel on behalf of Fortune Lewes complained that she is sick and weak and poor and wants some sustenance.

8/9/1733. Solomon Kenten and Mary Powel declared their intentions to marry. [They m. 7/12/1733.]

27/1/1734. Tuccohoe Meeting: Thomas Baynard being removed by death.

25/10/1734. James Wilson, Jr., complained that Samuel Dickenson accused him of perjury.

25/10/1734. John Ratclif and John Fellows intend to remove themselves and families in some part of the government of Carolina and desire certificates.

25/10/1734. Tucohoe Meeting: She that was the widow Susannah Baynard is m. by a priest.

*25/10/1734. John Kemp and Magdalen Stevens declared their intentions to marry. On 30/11/1734 they declared their intentions a second time and were given liberty to marry. On 26-27/12/1734 It was reported that the marriage of John Kemp had been accomplished in good order.

30/11/1734. Jacob Wooters informs the meeting that he with his family will remove to Carolina and requests a certificate.

30/11/1734. John Redgester intends to remove to Carolina and requests a certificate.

*30/11/1734. William Wilson and Rachel Baynard declared their intentions to marry. On 26/1/1735 the marriage of William Wilson was reported in pretty good order.

**26/12/1734. John Ball [of Kent Co., MD] and Jane Turner declared their intentions to marry. On 26-27/1/1735 they declared their intentions a second time and were given liberty to marry.

25/2/1734. George Baynard and Sussannah Powel, Jr., declared their intentions to marry.

*28/6/1734. Isaiah Parratt and Susannah Hopkins declared their intentions to marry. On 31/8/1734 the marriage of Isaiah Parratt was reported as accomplished in good order.

*28/6/1734. William Hopkins and Rebeckah Harwood declared their intentions to marry. On 31/8/1734 the marriage of William Hopkins was reported as accomplished in good order.

27/9/1734. Daniel Powel and Mary Sherwood declared their intentions to marry [with her father's consent]. [They m. 6/11/1734.]

29/11/1735. Reported that Elisabeth, widow of dec'd. Friend Jonathan Taylor was m. contrary to good order.

25/12/1735. John Stevens informed the meeting that Burtonwood Allcock is indebted to him and now he has obsconded.

25/12/1735. To visit her that was Elisabeth Atkinson.

25/12/1735. To visit her that was Sarah Harwood.

25/12/1735. To visit her that was Ann Edmondson.

25/12/1735. To visit her that was the widow Susannah Baynard.

25/12/1735. To visit her that was Leah Parrat.

25/12/1735. To visit her that was the widow Mary Ratclif.

31/5/1735. John Smith, late of Queen Anne's Co., by his last will, presented that the meeting take care that children, Michol and Mary Smith be brought up and educated as Quakers; they will remain under the care and tuition of Samuel Bartlet.

28/6/1735. Informed that Jeremiah Neel and his wife consented to their daughter being m. by a priest.

30/8/1735. A certificate of clearness in marriage was requested for Joseph Bartlet to be directed to Kent Co., MD.

*30/8/1735. Joseph Atkinson and Elisabeth Dixon declared their intentions to marry. On 31/10/1735 it was reported that the marriage of Joseph Atkinson was accomplished in good order.

31/1/1736. The bounds of the land of orphan Michol Smith were inspected and matters not appearing clear.

29/2/1736. Elizabeth Clayland, daughter of Thos. Atkinson condemned her disorderly marriage.

29/2/1736. Mary James, formerly Mary Ratclif, condemned her disorderly marriage.

29/2/1736. Elizabeth Clayland, daughter of Thos. Atkinson condemned her disorderly marriage.

24/9/1736. Thomas Stevens condemned his disorderly marriage.

26/11/1737. Samuel Bartlet passed his bond to the heirs of John Smith for £38.19.7 which was committed to the care of James Wilson, Jr. and James Berry.

28/2/1737. Tuckahoe Meeting: Elisabeth Buckenham has taken a husband by the priest.

*28/2/1737. Samuel Harwood and Francis Williams declared their intentions to marry. On ?/4/1737 it was reported that the marriage of Samuel Harwood was accomplished in good order.

25/3/1737. Treadhaven Meeting: Joanna, daughter of Francis Neall, has taken a husband contrary to good order.

?/4/1737. Tuckahoe Meeting: The widow Hannah Powel m. by a priest.

28/7/1737. Tuccohoe Meeting: Martha, daughter of Jacob Wotters, was m. by a priest.

28/7/1737. Reported that Kathrine Buckenham has begot a bastard child.

27/8/1737. There has been a difference between Joseph Derden and Isabel Tayler about the division of some land.

30/9/1737. Tuccohoe Meeting: Thomas Powel has m. by a priest.

30/9/1737. Treadhaven Meeting: Sarah Derden has gone to a priest for a husband.

1/11/1738. Howel Buckenham intends to proceed in marriage to a Friend in Kent Co., MD and desires a certificate.

28/12/1738. Bayside Meeting: Wm. Farebank has taken a wife by a priest.

28/12/1738. Isaac Milton of Kent Co., MD and Ann Bartlett declared their intentions to marry. [They m. 5/2/1739.]

28/12/1738. The meeting determines to move the orphan Michol Smith out of the possession of Samuel Bartlet and place him in the possession of John Cooper and said Cooper to take possession of the land.

31/3/1738. Consideration of the marriage of Elisabeth, daughter of James and Hannah Dickeson was before the meeting, finding that they as parents have not kept their authority therein, but have given their consent.

28/4/1738. William Thomas of Kent Co., MD and Joanna Powel declared their intentions to marry. [They m. 27/5/1738.]

30/6/1738. James Dickenson is now dec'd.; his widow will be visited regarding her daughter's marriage.

28/1/1739. Treadhaven Meeting: Sarah, daughter of Howel Powel has gone disorderly from her father and m. by a priest.

28/1/1739. It was reported that Mary, daughter of Hannah Dickenson, was m. by a priest. A committe to confer with Hannah Dickenson regarding her daughter Elizabeth's marriage.

26/2/1739. Wm. Farebanks [Fairbanks] has m. by a priest to his father's sister's daughter.

28/1/1739. Tuccohoe Meeting: Mary, widow of Robart Walker has been lately m. by a priest.

26/2/1739. Howel Powel for Howel Powel, Jr., informed the meeting that he intends to marry a woman of Kent Co. Monthly Meeting.

26/7/1739. James Racliff agrees to abide by the order of the meeting regarding him and his bro. Samuel [both of Talbot Co.].

26/7/1739. Peter Harwood and Joseph Derden were appointed to address the next court to give a remonstrance of the case of Edward Turner's children's estate.

1/9/1739. John Stewart of Anne Arundel Co. and Susannah Kemp of Talbot Co. declared their intentions to marry. On 28-29/9/1639 they declared their intentions a second time and were given liberty to marry.

26/1/1740. The meeting considers the disorderly marriage of Joanna, widow of William Thomas.

26/1/1740. John Webb and Grace Harwood declared their intentions to marry. [They m. 8/3/1740.]

1/3/1740. James Kemp being for sometime removed to the Western Shore did by some Friends request a certificate.

29/3/1740. Robart Jadwin applied for a certificate to be directed to the Captain of the militia in Queen Anne's Co.

25/4/1740. Henry Buckanham and Elisabeth Nox[?] declared their intentions to marry. [Henry Buckingham and Elizabeth Nicks of Talbot Co. m. 3/6/740.]

31/5/1740. Bayside Meeting: Thos. Kemp has lately m. by a priest.

31/5/1740. The meeting has concern for the religious education of Rachell, daughter of dec'd. Friend Jonathan Tayler, and the court proceedings thereon by appointing Thomas Bozman, guardian to the sd. orphan, who is not of our Society.

31/5/1740. Mary, daughter of John Farebank, has unlawfully begotten a child.

21/7/1740. A certificate is to be prepared for Henry Wood to be directed to the officers of the militia.

31/10/1741. William Williams and Elizabeth Harwood declared their intentions to marry [with consent of parents]. [They m. 2/12/1741.]

31/10/1741. George Nicks who has at times appeared at meetings for worship, asks to take a wife from among Friends.

24/12/1741. Tuckahoe Meeting: Thomas Powell has gone to the priest to be m.

30/2/1741. Thomas Ball, son of John Ball, has m. by a priest.

24/4/1741. Treadhaven Meeting: It was reported that Samuel Ratcliff has beat and abused his brother James.

24/4/1741. John Taylor produced a certificate from Bradshaw Hall Meeting in Comberland in Great Brittain dated 17/1/1740, directed to Friends in MD.

30/7/1741. Disorderly marriage by Joseph Atkinson.

30/7/1741. Consideration was made of Samuell Sharp who sometime past offered marriage to his mother's brother's daughter and have since m.

30/7/1741. The widow Isabel Taylor through sickness has become incapable of taking care of herself; the meeting agrees that her bro. Thomas Atkinson take her and her interest into his care; she is to be advised that if she lets her son spend her interest that Friends feel that they are not oblidged to maintain her.

30/7/1741. A disorderly marriage by Grace Webb [widow of Park Webb].

28/8/1741. John Walker, a member of the Society for sometime past is now suspected of divers and criminal cases.

28/8/1741. Benjamin Ball, not a member of the Society, complained against William Edmondson regarding the payment of old accounts [both are from Dorchester Co.].

28/8/1741. The disorderly marriage of Samuel Sharp and his wife is being considered.

29/10/1742. James Rattlife requested a certificate to the monthly meeting in Kent Co. on Delaware.

29/10/1742. The meeting considers the outrunning of the offspring of Thomas Baynard.

29/10/1742. John Regester requested a certificate to be directed to the monthly meeting in Kent Co. on Delaware, signifying his clearness in marriage.

29/10/1742. Elizabeth Stevens requested a certificate to Friends in Pennsylvania.

27/11/1742. Elizabeth Skilington haveing for sometime had encouragement from her relations in Barbadoes and she being desirious to go to that island, requested a certificate.

23/6/1742. Enoch Morgin and Sarah Neall declared their intentions to marry. [They m. 3/7/1742.]

28/8/1742. Samuell Duning requested a certificate to be directed to Kent Co., on Delaware.

1/1/1743. It is the judgment of the meeting that Susanna Powell should comply with her contract made with her daughter-in-law, Sarah Powell.

31/1/1743. John Baynard answered that he had been dilatory in attending meetings and as to living up according to what he professed he thought it impossible for one in his place of business. George Baynard answered that as to going to meetings he did not think it was worth his while to ride his horse to hear what was to be heard. Thomas Baynard's answer as to his marrying by a priest was that he was not sorry for it; Esther Baynard said that as to marrying by a priest she could not say she was sorry for it; Daborah Baynard said as to her going to a priest to be married, she thought if they had offered to be married in the meeting it would not be suffered.

31/1/1743. Timothy Hanson, Jr., and Elizabeth Skilington declared their intentions to marry. [They m. 20/2/1743.]

1/10/1743. Samuell Neall requested a certificate in relation to marriage, to be directed to the monthly meeting in Kent Co. on Delaware.

1/10/1743. Regarding Mary Dickinson, wife of Samuel who lived sometime in these parts and is now removed to Kent Co. on Delaware, the meeting thinks proper to have a certificate prepared for her.

29/10/1743. William Edmondson informed the meeting that there was a difference between Susanna Powell and his daughter Sarah Powell, late wife of Howell Powell, relating to her part of her husband's estate.

1/10/1743. A certificate was requested for Elizabeth Hanson.

26/11/1743. Tuckahoe Meeting: John Fooks has gone to a priest to be m.

29/2/1743. Treadhaven Meeting: John Harwood has gone to a priest to be m.

*29/2/1743. Howell Poweel [Powell] and Sarah Edmondson declared their intentions to marry. On 28/5/1743 the marriage of Howell Powell was reported as accomplished in good order.

29/2/1743. Francis Neall, Jr. requested a certificate in relation to marriage, to be directed to the monthly meeting in Kent Co. on Delaware.

28/5/1743. Mary Edmondson who wrote for the women's Friends has died.

1/7/1743. Bayside Meeting: Thomas Fairbanks seems willing to give satisfaction regarding his outgoing in marriage.

1/7/1743. William Gorsage and Hannah Dickenson have a difference regarding a note passed from James Dickinson [late husband of Hannah] to William Gorsage which said Hannah thinks not fit to pay until she has advice on the affair.

28/7/1743. Mary Webb has been m. by a priest.

28/7/1743. Tuckahoe Meeting: James Barnwell, Jr. has gone to a priest to be m.

**29/1/1744. Thomas Fooks and Elizabeth Anderson declared their intentions to marry. On 26/2/1744 the declared their intentions a second time and were given liberty to marry.

31/11/1744. Treadhaven Meeting: Robert Harwood, has m. by a priest.

31/11/1744. Lewis Clother has been very much reduced by fire; a collections will be made in each meeting for his relief.

27/4/1744. Rebecca Fooks condemned her disorderly walking.

26/5/1744. Peter Harwood, Jr., and Susanna Stuard declared their intentions to marry. [They m. 6/7/1744.]

25/7/1744. Isaac Williams and Lidia Harwood declared their intentions to marry. [They m. 7/9/1744.]

29/9/1744. Concern arose as to the likelihood of a difference between John Webb and the orphans of Peter Harwood, Jr.

?/5/1745. There is a difference betwixt Francis Neal and Edward Neal.

?/5/1745. The disorderly marriage of Joseph Durden is a concern.

*?/10/1744. George Reason and Sarah Powell declared their intentions to marry [with consent of parents]. On 31/11/1744 it was reported that the marriage of George Reason and Sarah Powell was accomplished in good order.

25/6/1745. There is a difference betwixt William Wilson and James Wilson.

*26/1/1746. Henry Heands and Rebecca Fooks declared their intentions to marry. On 28/3/1746 it was reported that the marriage of Henry Heands and Rebecca Fooks has been accomplished in good order.

26/1/1746. The lands of Thomas Taylor of Talbot Co., dec'd., have been divided by the meeting. The land consisted of 200 a. called Taylors Chance in the fork of Tuckahoe in QA Co.; also Turky Neck on Kings Neck in Talbot Co., reserving 125 a. which was sold to John Stacy, the whole containing 500 a.; also 2/3 of a tract called Kings Creek Marsh in Talbot Co. - in all containing 608 1/2 a. It was divided between John the elder who made choice of 200 a. called Taylors Chance and sold it, as also 100 a. out of Turky Neck. His bro. William was given the remainder. John died before it was made over. Some of his land was given to the daus.: Sarah Taylor (37 1/2 a.) and Rachel Taylor (37 1/2 a.).

1/10/1746. Wm. Hopkins has been reduced very low by sickness.

30/10/1745 [should read 1746]. William Taylor requested that the meeting divide the lands his father left his children according to his last will.

29/11/1746. A committee formed to resolve a difference between Edward Neel and Francis Neel, found it was about dividing some land that lay in Queen Anne's Co. near a place called Shadwell which land was called Shadwell's Addition, it being part of the said tract adjacent to Tuccahoe Creek. [*The committee made a division and described the bounds in the minutes.,*]

29/11/1746. The estate of Susannah Powel of Talbot Co. was divided as directed by her last will, and parts were designated to John Powel.

26/12/1746. William Edmondson has m. by a priest.

26/12/1746. The disorderly marriage of Solomon Harwood was reported.

28/3/1746. Joseph Durden condemned his disorderly marriage.

25/4/1746. The committee appointed to divide the lands [called Sybland near Hammonds Branch] of Ennion Williams, dec'd., among his five sons: William, Isaac, Joseph, Benjamin and Jobe, according to his last will has completed its work. [*A simple plat is included in the minutes*.]

25/4/1746. Sarah Wilson [Jr.] has married disorderly.

27/6/1746. Thomas Porter, guardian for Powel Cox, one of the legatees of Susannah Powel, dec'd., requested that the meeting appoint three Friends to divide her estate according to her last will.

24/7/1746. Henry Clark and Rebecca Cox declared their intentions to marry. [They m. 5/9/1746.]

24/7/1746. Henry Buckinham has m. by a priest.

24/7/1746. Daniel Dickinson requested a certificate relating to marriage [directed to Friends in Kent Co., MD].

27/9/1746. The marriage of Henry Clark was accomplished in good order.

30/10/1747. Informed that William Hopkins was very ill and in great poverty; a collection will be made.

30/10/1747. William Troth and Ann Birkhead declared their intentions to marry. [They m. 4/12/1747.]

30/10/1747. Tuccahoe Meeting: Rachael Thompson was m. by a priest.

*30/2/1747. Solomon Sharp and Ann Neel declared their intentions to marry. On 25/4/1747 it was reported that the marriage of Solomon Sharp and Ann Neel was accomplished in good order.

28/3/1747. The disorderly marriage of Isaac Dixon was reported.

26/9/1747. Samuel Sharp was removed by death.

31/1/1748. Elizabeth Stevens has a mind to remove to Philadelphia and requests a certificate.

26/8/1748. James Wilson, Jr., and Jane Clark declared their intentions to marry. [They m. 8/10/1748.]

29/11/1749. Joseph Williams and Abigail Clark declared their intentions to marry. [They m. 28/12/1749.]

26/12/1749. Michael Smith, orphan of John Smith was put into the care and tuition of Samuel Bartlet and the said Samuel having refused to educate him according to the truth by the Society proposed, Isaac Williams was appointed to take care of the orphan and to school and cloath him until he reaches the age of 21.

26/2/1749. James Kemp and Elizabeth Williams declared their intentions to marry. [They m. 2/4/1749.]

28/4/1749. A certificate is to be prepared for Powel Cox relating to his clearness in marriage, to be directed to Kent Co., MD.

*27/7/1749. Samuel Harwood and Elisabeth Clayland declared their intentions to marry. On 27/9/1749 it was reported that the marriage of Samuel Harwood and Elisabeth Clayland was accomplished in good order.

30/8/1749. A certificate is to be prepared for Elisabeth Edmondson relating to clearness in marriage and clearness in conversation.

26/1/1750. The marriage of Joseph Williams and Abigail Clark was accomplished in good order.

26/1/1750. The meeting having under consideration the disorderly behavior of Samuel Bartlet and his leaving the meeting in such abrupt a manner.

28/11/1750. The will of Thomas Atkinson was produced to the meeting and a committee appointed to divide his estate among his children in accordance with the will.

28/11/1750. William Troth intends to remove from this Province and settle in Wilmington; he requested a certificate for himself and wife, to be directed to the Wilmington Monthly Meeting.

30/5/1750. Edward Clark and Johannah Allcock declared their intentions to marry. [They m. 28/6/1750.]

28[?]/6/1750. A difference has arisen between John Berry as exec. of John Taylor and William Troth as attorney for Elizabeth Stevens [of the City of Philadelphia, widow].

30/10/1751. Joseph Berry and Sarah Cockayne declared their intentions to marry. [They m. 27/1/1752.]

*30/10/1751. Samuel Harwood, Jr., and Sarah Atkinson declared their intentions to marry. On 24/2/1752 it was reported that he marriage of Samuel Harwood and Sarah Atkinson was accomplished but not so orderly as could be desired through a too hasty proceeding.

30/10/1751. William Troth produced a certificate for Solomon Neal directed to the monthly meeting at Duck Creek.

*29/5/1751. Isaac Turner and Hannah Bartlet declared their intentions to marry. On 30/7/1751 it was reported that the marriage of Isaac Turner and Hannah Bartlet was accomplished in good order.

29/5/1751. William Troth declined removing to Wilmington.

26/6/1751. Mary Clark has m. by a priest.

28/8/1751. A certificate was requested for Solomon Neal to the monthly meeting at Kent Co. on Delaware.

28/8/1751. Disorderly marriages of Isaac Cox and Daniel Bartlet were reported.

27/11/1752. A committee has divided the land of James Berry among his four sons [*platt shown in minutes*].

*25/12/1752. Job Williams and Rachel Harwood declared their intentions to marry. On 26/2/1753 it was reported that the marriage of Job Williams and Rachel Harwood was accomplished in good order.

25/12/1752. Stephen Ratcliff condemned his disorderly marriage.

25/12/1752. Samuel Harwood, Jr. condemned his and his wife's disorderly practice before marriage.

24/2/1752. James Wilson informed the meeting that his son Thomas Wilson intends to remove out of this Province and settle in Kent Co. on Delaware and requests a certificate.

30/3/1752. The disorderly marriage of William Atkinson was reported.

29/6/1752. The orphans of John Smith who were left to the care of the monthly meeting are now of age and desiring their estate left by their father.

31/8/1752. Informed that Edward Neal took a mare which was proved in court to belong to another man and while in his custody she was mismarked.

29/10/1753. Certificates were requested for Jonathan Neal and John Jenkinson to monthly meeting at Nottingham, relating to their educations and clearness in marriage.

29/10/1753. Obadiah Atkinson and Elizabeth Harwood declared their intentions to marry. [They m. 27/11/1753.]

29/10/1753. Daniel Hull who formerly dwelt in Kent Co., MD, did lately come and settle in Talbot Co. without producing a certificate though it was requested of him and having brought a scandal by contracting debts beyond his ability to pay.

29/10/1753. Edward Clark states that he was very willing that his wife come back again and live with him; she writes that she never intends to live with her husband let the consequence be what it will.

29/10/1753. A certificate was requested for Aaron Atkinson certifying his clearness in mariage, to be directed to Nottingham Monthly Meeting.

26/11/1753. Henry Clark and Jane Atkinson declared their intentions to marry. [They m.1/1/1754.]

31/12/1753. A difference has arisen betwen Isaac Williams and John Berry [Isaac Williams sent Berry a letter giving advice in a very friendly loving manner and Berry replied with divers false charges].

26/2/1753. Joseph Berry condemned his and his wife's disorderly practice before marriage.

26/2/1753. Thomas Atkinson requested a certificate for his brother Aaron Atkinsson, to be directed to the monthly meeting at East Nottingham in Chester Co.

26/2/1753. James Ratcliff, son of William Ratcliff intends to settle in North Carolina within the verge of Falling Creek Monthly Meeting; he requested a certificate.

30/4/1753. Tuccaho Meeting: Reported the disorderly practice of Edward Clark and his wife's living separate; Friends' efforts to reconcile them has been ineffectual [she now lives at a great distance].

25/6/1753. William Webb and Lydia Cowgill declared their intentions to marry. [They m.1/8/1753.]

25/6/1753. Tuccaho Meeting reported the disorderly marriage of John Berry.

25/2/1754. The disorderly marriage of Solomon Neal was reported.

29/4/1754. Treadhaven Meeting: The disorderly marriage of Peter Harwood, Jr. reported.

29/4/1754. Tuccaho Meeting: Benjamin Williams in his life and conversation has become a scandal to Truth.

27/5/1754. Isaac Turner and his wife were too freely accompanying together before marriage.

27/5/1754. The disorderly marriage of Hannah [Johannah] Clark reported; she does not intend to give any satisfaction.

24/6/1754. Tuccahoe Meeting reports the extravagantcy of Job Williams in his way of living and superfluity of apparel.

24/6/1754. Peter Harwood, Jr., and his wife confess their sorrow for their disorderly marriage by a priest, being too near a kin and too conversant together before marriage.

29/7/1754. To visit Powel Cox in regard to his disorderly marriage [also proceeding too soon after the death of his wife's formerl husband].

26/8/1754. James Wilson, Jr. and his wife promise to be be more diligent in attending meetings in the future.

30/9/1754. Isaac Williams complained that Samuel Harwood, Sr., is indebted to him as guardian to his sister Margaret Williams which he delays to pay.

27/1/1755. Benjamin Parratt and Mary Ann Wilson declared their intentions to marry. [They m. 5/3/1755.]

27/1/1755. It is the judgment of the meeting that John Berry acted contrary to Discipline in having Elisabeth Stevens arrested when she was down at the Yearly.

*27/10/1755. John George and Rachel Wilson declared their intentions to marry. On 26/1/1756 it was reported that the marriage of John George and Rachel Wilson was accomplished in good order.

27/10/1755. Howell Powel condemned his disorderly marriage.

24/2/1755. Johanna Clark refused to repent.

24/2/1755. John Berry states he had Elisabeth Stevens arrested in order to bring her to an arbitration; he acknowledges that he was wrong to do so; the meeting will write her to say that they think she should meet him half way and settle their differances.

31/3/1755. Elizabeth Stevens writes she does not intend to comply with the meeting's request.

26/5/1755. Jonathan Neal informed the meeting that Stephen Ratcliff has sued him with a provincial writt for a part of his wife's portion that was due to him notwithstanding he had offered to settle the said difference and to pay off the said estate and to abide the judgment of arbitrators.

30/6/1755. Joseph Williams intends to remove to Nottingham and requested a certificate [with wife].

30/6/1755. A child of Job Williams has become an object of charity.

25/8/1755. Friends are dissatisified concerning William Taylor's keeping Rebekah Hanes about his house from a suspicion of their being too intimately concerned with each other. [They refused to separate at first but later agreed to live apart.]

25/8/1755. Benjamin Folks informed the meeting that he had been called upon to bear arms and requested a certificate to satisfy the officers [Dorchester Co.].

29/9/1755. Women Friends have visited Elizabeth Parratt in regard to her disorderly marriage; she doesn't seem inclined to give Friends any satisfaction.

26/1/1756. William Taylor and Rebeckah Hanes have come together again contrary to the advice of this meeting.

25/10/1756. Informed that James Ratcliff has advised his son not to settle the difference between him and Jonathan Neal.

29/11/1756. Daniel Powell has had a disorderly marriage.

29/11/1756. James Bartlett, Jr. has a disorderly marriage.

29/11/1756. Marshe Creek Meeting: John Edmondson, Jr. has m. by a priest.

*23/3/1756. Peter Edmondson and Sophia Neall declared their intentions to marry. On 26/4/1756 it was reported that the marriage of Peter Edmondson and Sophia Neall was accomplished in good order.

26/4/1756. Choptank Meeting: The disorderly marriage of Rebecca Fairbanks was reported.

31/5/1756. Isaac Cox and Rachel Atkinson declared their intentions to marry. [They m. 1/7/1756.]

31/5/1756. Tuckahoe Meeting: The disorderly marriage of Edward Clark, Jr. was reported.

31/5/1756. Aaron Atkinson produced a certificate from the monthly meeting at

East Nottingham relating his clearness in marriage.

31/5/1756. Edward Clark, Jr. confemned his disorderly marriage.

31/5/1756. Wm. Hopkins is still in a helpless condition.

26/7/1756. The disorderly marriage of Willm. Edmondson was reported.

*31/1/1757. Jonathan Neall, Jr., produced a certificate from East Nottingham Monthly Meeting signifying his clearness in marriage.

*31/1/1757. John Dixon and Eliza: Kemp the younger declared their intentions to marry. On 28/3/1757 it was reported that the marriage of John Dixon and Eliza: Kemp was accomplished in good order.

28/2/1757. The disorderly marriage of James Rattcliff, Jr. was reported.

28/2/1757. Isaac Williams intends to remove to Pennsylvania with his family and requests a certificate for himself and wife, to be directed to East Nottingham Meeting.

28/3/1757. William Taylor and Eliza: Edmondson, Jr., declared their intentions to marry. [They m. 20/4/1757.]

28/3/1757. The disorderly marriage of Peter Rattclif was reported.

30/1/1758. John Jenkinson produced a certificate from the monthly meeting at East Nottingham, relating his clearness in marriage.

30/1/1758. Joseph Berry requested a certificate for Benjamin Berry to the monthly meeting at Little Creek in Kent Co. upon Delaware.

30/1/1758. Daniel Powell, treasurer, was removed by death.

27/3/1758. Thomas Atkinson condemned his disorderly marriage.

27/3/1758. Elizabeth Edmondson requested a certificate to the monthly meeting at Philadelphia.

26/8/1758. A difference arose between John Catrop and Francis Neal, both of Talbot Co. regarding land which Catrop rented from Neal.

26/8/1758. John Webb had a disorderly marriage.

*25/9/1758. Peter Webb and Sarah Anderson declared their intentions to marry. [They m. 4/11/1758.]

29/1/1759. Emanuel Jenkinson requested a certificate to the monthly meeting in

Kent Co., MD, certifying his clearness in marriage.

29/1/1759. Informed of the disorderly marriage of Danll. Bartlett.

29/1/1759. A collection was made for Rebeckah Hopkins, widow, who is burdened with children.

29/11/1759. John Edmondson applied for a certificate for his son Sollomon Edmondson, to be directed to the Wilmington Monthly Meeting.

26/2/1759. Informed that Thos. Stevens and Henry Dickinson are leading lost and libertine ways.

26/2/1759. Dennis Hopkins requested to come under the care of Friends.

26/2/1759. A certificate was received for Henry Coventry, his wife and children, Jno. George and wife, Joseph Gill, Steven Gudgian, John and Richard Swift, Mary Wright, widow of Nathan Wright and Sarah Baynard, wife of Nathan Baynard.

26/2/1759. Kesiah Neal received permission to take such measures as the law directs to recover a Negro lately taken from her.

26/3/1759. Friends were appointed to assist Rebeckah Hopkins in getting places to bind out her children.

26/3/1759. Solomon Neal requests to be taken under the care of Friends.

26/3/1759. Informed of the disorderly marriage of Wm. Dickinson.

29/11/1759. Testification against Thos. Steavens stating he has allowed fiddling and dancing and also puppets to be shown in his house.

30/4/1759. Informed of the disorderly marriage of Daniel Cox.

31/1/1760. Wm. Gudgion requested a certificate to Kent Co. (MD) to certify his clearness in marriage.

*27/11/1760. George Willson and Sarah Baynard, Jr. declared their intentions to marry. On 27/1/1761 it was reported that the marriage of George Willson and Sarah Baynard was accomplished in good order.

27/11/1760. Marshe Creek Meeting reports that Francis Edmondson leads a disorderly life in keeping bad company, horse racing and fighting.

28/2/1760. Henry Dickinson has been guilty of gaming, horse racing and disorderly conversation and does not make satisfaction.

28/2/1760. The disorderly marriage of Wm. Rattcliff was reported.

31/7/1760. Benjamin Berry produced a certificate from the monthly meeting of Duck Creek signifying his clearness in marriage.

27/8/1760. William Ratcliff appeared and condemned his disorder in being married to his cousin by a priest.

26/11/1761. Testimony against Elizabeth Smith.

26/11/1761. Francis Neal unable to attend the meeting because of sickness.

26/11/1761. Marshe Creek reported the disorderly marriage of Thos. Edmondson.

26/3/1761. Lambert Hopkins to be visited regarding his disorderly marriage.

30/4/1761. John Jenkinson and Mary Covinton declared their intentions to marry. [They m. 29/5/1761.]

30/4/1761. Thomas Cockayne requested a certificate to the monthly meeting at Duck Creek in Kent Co. upon Delaware.

30/4/1761. Bayside Meeting reports the disorderly marriage of Benjamin Kemp, it being the second time he has been guilty of the same disorder and never dealt with for the first.

30/4/1761. Third Haven reports the disorderly practice of James Webb in drinking to excess.

28/5/1761. The women Friends produced a testimony against Hannah Neal.

28/5/1761. James Berry produced a paper condemning his and his wife's disorderly practices.

28/5/1761. The women Friends produced a testimony against Rebecca Walker.

28/5/1761. A certificate was produced for Friend Esther Bartlett to Wilmington Monthly Meeting.

25/6/1761. A certificate was requested for Isaac Cox, Jr. to be directed to Duck Creek Monthly Meeting in Kent Co. upon Delaware.

25/6/1761. A certificate for Rebecca Tucker to West River Monthly Meeting.

25/6/1761. A certificate for Martha Neal to monthly meeting at Little Creek in Kent Co. (DE).

29/7/1761. A certificate was produced for Elizabeth Maxfield directed to the monthly meeting at Little Creek in Kent Co. on Delaware.

30/7/1761. The women Friends produced a testimony against Sarah Kirby.

30/7/1761. The women Friends produced a testimony against Ann Allford.

30/7/1761. Jonathan Neal requested a certificate to Cecil Monthly Meeting.

30/7/1761. James Webb condemned his disorder in drinking to excess.

30/7/1761. The women Friends produced a testimony against Kesiah Burges.

27/8/1761. Daniel Hull produced a paper condemning his disorderly practices.

28/1/1762. John Gill produced a certificate from the monthly meeting at Aldston in Cumberland.

28/10/1762. Wm. Wilson denies that he appeared in a spirit of anger at meetings and that he opposed nothing but what he thought was wrong.

25/11/1762. A certificate was requested for Willm. Troth and his sons, Henry and William.

25/11/1762. Rebecca Clark has left a legacy to Friends of Tuckaho Meeting to be applied to repairing their graveyard.

30/12/1762. The meeting was informed that Samuel Harwood 3d, an apprentice to James Ball, is under the hands of a Doctor by the direction of the court, which is not to the satisfaction of Friends; it will be determined if his master will deliver him into the hands of Friends.

30/12/1762. Benjamin Berry requested permission to take the measures the law directs to condemn a piece of ground in order to build a water mill thereon.

30/12/1762. John Edmondson, Jr., and Mary Neal declared their intentions to marry. [They m. 28/1/1763.]

30/12/1762. Jonathan Neal and Sarah Willson, Jr., declared their intentions to marry. [They m. 2/2/1763.]

30/12/1762. Aaron Parratt and Mary Neal, Jr., declared their intentions to marry. [They m. 31/3/1763.]

25/3/1762. Bayside Meeting reports the disorderly marriage of Thomas Kemp.

27/4/1762. Concern is given to the children of John Webb; they are likely to suffer and their mother is willing to give them up to Friends.

24/6/1762. Jonathan Neal produced a certificate from the monthly meeting in Kent Co. signifying his clearness in marriage.

26/8/1762. Thomas Cockayne produced a certificate from the monthly meeting of Duck Creek in Kent Co. on Delaware signifying his clearness in marriage.

26/8/1762. The eldest child of John Webb has been placed with John Jenkinson and the youngest with James Bartlett and they are to have £8 per year.

30/9/1762. Friends visited James Willson [regarding his appearing in anger at meetings]; he told them that he intended not to sett in Preparative Meetings of business for the future, for if he saw things he could not help opposing.

27/1/1763. It was reported that Willm. Ratcliff's life and conversation is such as Friends cannot have unity with, he having frequently drank to excess.

29/12/1763. Testification was made against Elizabeth Jenkinson (now Laine).

29/12/1763. Testification was made against Sarah Hopkins, Jr.

29/12/1763. Testification was made against Rebecca Taylor.

29/12/1763. Testification was made against Sarah Bartlett (now Hopkins).

24/2/1763. The disorderly marriage of Joshua Clark, Jr. was reported.

24/2/1763. John Kemp, Jr., and Mary Wrightson declared their intentions to marry. [They m. 7/4/1763.]

31/3/1763. Garratt Sipple of Kent Co. on Delaware and Elizabeth Berry declared their intentions to marry. [They m. 29/4/1763.]

31/3/1763. Samuel Rowland of Sussex Co. on Delaware and Mary Wright declared their intentions to marry. [They m. 2/6/1763.] On 30/6/1763 it was reported that the marriage of Samuel Rowland and Mary Wright had been accomplished but not in so good order as could have been desired by reason of a disorderly person coming into the meeting and making some disturbance.

28/4/1763. Clayton Cowgill of Kent Co., on Delaware and Martha Neal declared their intentions to marry. [They m. 27/5/1763.]

28/4/1763. James Ratcliffe has for some time past neglected to attend meetings for worship and freuqently drank to excess.

28/4/1763. James Webb has removed from Third Haven to Tuckaho Meeting.

26/5/1763. Joseph Atkinson and Elizabeth Neal, Jr. declared their intentions to

marry. [They m. 1/7/1763.]

30/6/1763. A certificate was produced for Elizabeth Sipple to the monthly meeting in KE Co on Delaware.

30/6/1763. Samuel Harwood, the 3d is removed by death; the expences from his board have already been paid by his relations.

28/7/1763. A certificate was produced for Mary Thomas, directed to the monthly meeting in Kent Co. (MD).

28/7/1763. The disorderly marriage of John Hopkins was reported.

29/9/1763. The disorderly marriage of Dennis Hopkins, Jr. was reported; disowned.

29/9/1763. A certificate for Mary Rowland was produced, directed to the monthly meeting in Kent Co. on Delaware.

29/9/1763. A place was sought to board out the orphan John Webb; James Berry has taken him.

26/1/1764. A certificate was produced for Martha Cowgill, directed to the monthly meeting in Kent Co. on Delaware.

29/11/1764. Solomon Edmondson produced a certificate from Wilmington Monthly Meeting signifying his clearness in marriage.

27/12/1764. Henry Troth having lately removed with his family within the verge of this meeting, produced a certificate from Wilmington Monthly Meeting for himself, his wife Sarah, and their children: William, Samuel, Henry, John and Elizabeth.

29/3/1764. Tuckaho Meeting reports that Enoch Morgan has for a long time neglected attending meetings and has been guilty of drinking to excess.

26/4/1764. A testification was produced against Mary Silvester (formerly Williams).

31/5/1764. Thomas Cockayne and Sarah Kemp declared their intentions to marry. [They m. 5/7/1764.]

31/5/1764. A testification was produced against Sarah Ratcliff, wife of William Ratcliff.

20/6/1764. Thomas Cockayne has lately suffered much loss by fire; a collection will be made.

20/6/1764. A testification was made Rachel Edmondson, formerly Williams.

27/9/1764. John Gill produced a paper condemning his drinking to excess.

31/10/1765. Henry Sherwood and Elizabeth Williams declared their intentions to marry. [They m. 29/11/1765.]

28/11/1765. Isaac Williams requested a certificate for Elizabeth Williams, daughter of Job Williams, directed to Nottingham Monthly Meeting.

26/12/1765. Marshe Creek Meeting reported Solomon Edmondson being m. contrary to good order and amongst Friends [by a magistrate]; disowned.

*28/2/1765. Thomas Norris, Jr. of West River, and Mary Kemp declared their intentions to marry. On 25/4/1765 it was reported that tthe marriage of Thomas Norris, Jr. and Mary Kemp had been accomplished in good order.

28/3/1765. Aron Atkinson informed the meeting that by the last will of his dec'd. father and mother [Thomas and Rachel Atkinson] the monthly meeting was vested with the power to settle the estate amongst the children.

30/5/1765. William Troth has lately removed within the verge of this meeting and produced a certificate from the Wilmington Monthly Meeting for himself, his wife Lydia and their children: Henry, William and Hannah.

30/5/1765. A certificate for Mary Norris was produced.

30/5/1765. The disorderly practice of Joseph Gill in drinking to excess was reported.

30/5/1765. Powel Cox requested leave of the meeting to sell some Negroes who had fallen into his lands by means of an attachment. [This was approved with the understanding that he would get good places for them.]

25/7/1765. David Corse of Kent Co. (MD) and Elizabeth Fairbank declared their intentions to marry. [They m. 31/8/1765.]

29/8/1765. In the settlement of the estate of the Atkinsons, James Ratcliffe one of the trustees, was dead by this date; Isaac Williams had removed out of the Province. It was judged by the committee that either Obadiah Atkinson or Aaron Atkinson possess the land and pay the other the sum of £233.15.0.

30/1/1766. John Register and Esther Willson declared their intentions to marry. [They m. 28/2/1766.]

30/1/1766. Thomas Willson and Lydia Register declared their intentions to marry. [They m. 3/3/1766.]

30/10/1766. Thirdhaven Meeting reported that Dennis Hopkins, Sr. had sold a Negro slave to Daniel Bartlett.

25/12/1766. George Browning and Margret Neal declared their intentions to marry. A certificate was received for him from Kent Co. Monthly Meeting. [They m. 30/1/1767.]

25/12/1766. Powel Cox requested a certificate for his son David Cox whom he has placed as an apprentice at Wilmington.

25/12/1766. A certificate was produced for Elizabeth Corse directed to the monthly meeting in Kent Co.

27/2/1766. The life and conversation of Edward Clerk, Jr. appears to be in a good degree orderly.

27/2/1766. A testification was produced against Sarah Scott, formerly Webb.

26/6/1766. Tuckaho Meeting reports that William Parrat has m. by a priest; disowned.

31/7/1766. Daniel Smith having lately removed within the verge of the meeting produced a certificate from the monthly meeting at Cape May dated 26/6/1766.

28/8/1766. Thirdhaven Meeting reports that Robert Neal has for some time past led a disorderly life and has of late been guilty of swearing and fighting.

28/8/1766. Elizabeth Edmondson who removed from hence to Philadelphia some years past, obtained a certificate from the meeting dated 4th month 1758 and lately removed back within the verge of this meeting, she producing the same certificate having not delivered it according to the intent thereof.

28/8/1766. A testification was produced against Frances Register.

26/11/1767. John Jenkinson produced an account against the meeting for the maintenance of the children of John Webb, dec'd., and as the mother has denied Friends the priviledge of educating them, the meeting will ask to receive from her a sum to defray the said charges.

26/11/1767. Robert George of Kent Co. and Ann Edmondson [Choptank Meeting] declared their intentions to marry. [They m. 1/1/1768.]

26/11/1767. Thirdhaven Meeting offers that Francis Hopkins has m. by a priest; disowned.

26/11/1767. John Gill having removed to Philadelphia some years past without requesting a certificate; one was to be sent.

31/12/1767. Daniel Willson and Rebecca Barnwell declared their intentions to marry. [They m. 29/1/1768.]

31/12/1767. James Berry requested a certificate signifying his clearness in marriage to be directed to Duck Creek Monthly Meeting.

26/3/1767. A certificate was produced for Margaret Browning directed to Cecil Monthly Meeting.

26/3/1767. A testification was produced against Martha Jordan.

30/4/1767. Marshee Creek Meeting offers that James Edmondson requests to be under the care of Friends.

28/5/1767. Solomon Hopkins having accomplished his marriage by a priest was disowned.

30/7/1767. Joseph Berry produced certificates of manumission for Negroes Abram and Hannah, and a bond on himself and heirs to sett Negro Philip free when he arrives at the age of 21.

30/7/1767. A certificate was produced for Rachel Edmondson directed to the monthly meeting at Little Creek.

22/8/1767. Thirdhaven Meeting reported that Samuel Register had accomplished his marriage by a priest.

22/8/1767. It was reported that Robert Neal has been guilty of keeping unprofitable company and taking other undue liberties; disowned.

22/8/1767. Benjamin Berry produced a bond obliging himself to sett the following Negroes, now minors, free: Edward, by 25/12/1777; Rachel by 18/2/1785; and Hannah by 18/2/1779.

22/8/1767. It was reported that Benja. Kemp has of late been guilty of profane swearing.

24/9/1767. It was reported that Joseph Atkinson at divers times has been a good deal elevated with liquor and of late in the practice of excessive drinking; disowned.

28/1/1768. John Edmndson, Jr. having removed with his family and settled within the verge of Duck Creek Monthly Meeting, requested a certificate.

27/10/1768. Peter Sharp for whom a testification was being prepared, has since removed by death.

24/11/1768. A testification was produced against Mary Atkinson formerly Bartlett.

25/2/1768. A certificate was produced for Ann George directed to the monthly meeting in Kent Co.

25/2/1768. A certificate was requested for Jonathan Neal for himself, wife and children, to be directed to Duck Creek Monthly Meeting.

31/3/1768. William Clark has m. by a priest; disowned.

31/3/1768. Daniel Smith removed by death.

31/3/1768. Tuckahoe Meeting reports that Samuel Harwood, Jr. has m. by a priest; disowned.

20/4/1768. A testification was produced against Mary Claypole, formerly Harwood.

26/5/1768. Henry Troth and Sarah Smith request leave to take legal measures to collect some debts due them.

30/6/1768. George Willson will be treated with regard to his buying a Negro slave.

28/7/1768. Susanna Berry, wife of James Berry, having lately removed and settled within the verge of Thirdhaven Monthly Meeting, produced a certificate from Duck Creek Monthly Meeting.

28/7/1768. Ann Powel, wife of Howel Powell, was received into membership.

29/9/1768. Peter Sharp has accomplished his marriage by a priest; disowned.

29/9/1768. Samuel Hanson, Jr. of Kent Co. on Delaware and Lydia Berry declared their intentions to marry. [They m. 28/10/1768.]

29/9/1768. A certificate for Jonathan Neal, his wife Sarah and their children: Ann and James, was produced.

26/1/1769. John Stuard intends to proceed in marriage with a member of Cecil Monthly Meeting and requests a certificate.

26/1/1769. A certificate was produced for Lydia Hanson directed to Duck Creek Monthly Meeting.

26/1/1769. Benjamin Berry produced manumissions and certificates for nine Negroes: Joe, Bassy, Edward, Lucy, Henny, Rachel, Hannah, Meniors[?] and

Esther.

26/10/1769. William Edmondson and Sarah Smith declared their intentions to marry. [They m. 6/12/1769.]

26/10/1769. Queen Anne's Meeting reports that Christopher Willson has accomplished his marriage by a priest.

26/10/1769. Thirdhaven Meeting offers that Powell Cox has suffered a courtship to be carried on to his daughter-in-law Elizabeth Sharp whose marriage was accomplished by a priest at his house.

23/2/1769. A testification was produced against Rachel Ferriss, late Willson.

*23/2/1769. Thirdhaven Meeting reports that Henry Troth and Elizabeth Neal declare their intentions to marry. On 27/3[should read 4]/1769 it was reported that the marriage of Henry Troth and Elizabeth Neal had been accomplished in good order.

23/2/1769. Benjamin Berry declared his intention to marry and requested a certificate to be directed to Philadelphia Monthly Meeting.

23/2/1769. A testification was produced against Sarah Manship, late Webb.

30/3/1769. Elizzbeth Neal manumitted Negroes James Commons and Murreah.

30/3/1769. Isaac Dixon produced an account of four cattle executed from him for priests' demands and church rates (so called).

30/3/1769. A testification was produced against Elizabeth Dickinson, late Sharp.

30/3/1769. Thirdhaven Meeting reports that Robert Harwood, Jr. has m. by a priest; disowned.

25/5/1769. A testification was produced against Deborah Jones, late Hopkins.

29/6/1769. Isaac Cox reported one gun confiscated from him for priests demand.

27/7/1769. John Stuard having removed to Kent Co. (MD) requested a certificate be directed to Cecil Monthly Meeting.

31/8/1769. William Troth reported a cow was confiscated from him in 1768 for priests' demand and church rates, so called.

31/8/1769. Sarah Berry, wife of Benjamin Berry, having lately removed into the area, produced a certificate from Philadelphia Monthly Meeting.

28/9/1769. Joseph Berry reported one pair of steelyards confiscated for priests' demands and church rates.

28/9/1769. William Edmondson produced an account of 11/3 detained from him by the sheriff for priests' demands.

28/9/1769. Isaac Dixon produced an account of four cattle confiscated from him for a claim in 1762, 63 and 64 for priests' demands and church rates.

28/9/1769. Thomas Cockayne produced an account of one pair of saddle baggs confiscated for priests' demands.

25/1/1770. William Willson, Jr., and Ann Kemp declared their intentions to marry. [They m. 27/2/1770 at Bayside.]

25/1/1770. Powel Cox requested a certificate for his son Daniel Powel Cox, to be directed to Duck Creek Monthly Meeting.

29/11/1770. Choptank Meeting reported the disorderly conduct of Kinsey Edmondson in frequent gaming.

27/12/1770. Thirdhaven Meeting offered that Samuel Neal has m. by a priest.

27/12/1770. Nicholas, Edward and Sarah Cox, children of Powel and Ann Cox have a birth right among Freidns and are removed with their said parents to Kent Co. on Delaware; a certificate will be prepared for them.

22/2/1770. Isaac Dixon produced manumissions for three slaves: James, Phillis and Moll.

22/2/1770. Benjamin Parvin of Pennsylvania and Sarah Powell declared their intentions to marry, he producing a certificate from Exeter Monthly Meeting. [They m. 3/4/1770.]

22/2/1770. Daniel Clerk having been m. by a priest to a person not of our Society; disowned.

26/4/1770. A testification was produced against Deborah Baggs late Coventon.

26/4/1770. A testification was produced against Rebecca Catrop, late Harwood.

26/4/1770. Danil Dickinson requested a certificate for his son John, to be directed to the monthly meeting at Wilmington.

26/6/1770. Edward Clark has purchased a Negro slave.

26/6/1770. Henry Troth requested a certificate for his son William, to be directed to the monthly meeting at Philadelphia, and one for his son Samuel to the monthly meeting at Wilmington.

26/7/1770. A testimony was produced against Ann Cox.

26/7/1770. Katharine Lightfoot who formerly resided at Philadelphia having removed within the verge of Thirdhaven Monthly Meeting, produced a certificate from monthly meeting at Philadelphia.

30/8/1770. Thirdhaven Meeting offered that William Dixon has accomplished his marriage by a priest; disowned.

30/8/1770. Tuckaho Meeting offered that William Wilson, Jr. had been active in the purchase of a Negro slave.

30/8/1770. Edward Clerk acknowledged his sorrow in purchasing a Negro child contrary to the advice of Friends; he stated he would not have done it except to keep it from being separated from its mother.

27/9/1770. William Edmondson manumitted a Negro man named Isaac.

27/9/1770. The Philadelphia Monthly Meeting testified against Elizabeth Edmondson.

27/9/1770. James Edmondson manumitted a Negro man named Nero.

28/2/1771. Thomas Kemp accomplished his marriage by a priest.

28/2/1771. William Troth requested a certificate for his son Henry Troth, Jr. who had removed to Kent Co.

28/3/1771. A certificate for Elizabeth Berry, daughter of John Berry, dec'd., directed to Duck Creek Monthly Meeting.

28/3/1771. A testimony was produced against Sarah Thomas, late Berry.

25/4/1771. Sarah Register manumitted Jacob and Jane.

25/4/1771. Benjamin Parvin manumitted Adam, Eve, Isaac, Phill and Peggy.

25/4/1771. Sarah Powel manumitted Jude, Jimy, Minta and Rose.

25/4/1771. Aaron Adkisson produced a certificate from the monthly meeting of Salem in New England signifying his clearness of marriage engagements.

25/4/1771. James Berry manumitted Harry, Swirn[Iwirn?], George, Peter, David, Lucy, Memory and Rhoda.

30/5/1771. Testimony against Kinsey Edmondson.

30/5/1771. Mary Adkinson acknowledges her outgoing in marriage.

27/6/1771. Women Friends produced a certificate of removal for Sarah Pervin [Parvin] wife of Benjamin Parvin, to be directed to Wilmington Monthly Meeting.

27/6/1771. Isaac Cox informed the meeting that he intended a journey to the warm springs in Virginia and desires the concurrence of the meeting and the meeting concurs and desires his welfare and safe return.

25/7/1771. Henry Troth having placed his son Henry an apprentice in Philadelphia requests that a few lines be sent to Philadelphia Monthly Meeting.

29/8/1771. Henry Morgin will be visited regarding his disorderly conduct. On 1/10/1771 he was disowned.

29/8/1771. William Edmondson requests to taken leave to take the measures the law directs to recover some debts due from persons not of our Society.

26/9/1771. Aaron Adkinson and Ann Dixon declare their intentions of marriage. [They m. 11/4/1771.]

26/9/1771. Women Friends produced a certificate for Susannah Train directed to Duck Creek Monthly Meeting.

26/9/1771. William Troth and Obediah Adkinson produced accounts of their sufferings for priest demands and church rates so-called.

26/8/1771. Francis Edmondson produced a paper condemning his disorder. On 30/11/1775 Francis Edmndson was disowned.

26/8/1711. Thomas Cockayn requests leave to take measures the law directs to recover a debt due to him from a person not of our Society.

28/11/1771. John George requests leave to take measures the law directs to recover some debts due him from persons not of our Society.

27/2/1772. Benjamin Williams requests that his father's Will be complied with in regard to his lands.

3?/3/1772. A certificate was received on behalf of Rachel [?] Edmondson, wife of Francis Edmondson from Duck Creek Meeting.

3?/3/1772. John Edmondson of Kent Co. on Delaware and Esther Bartlett declared their intentions of marriage; he is requested to present a certificate from his monthly meeting. [They m. 1/5/1772.]

3?3/1772. Certificates of removal were received from Cecil Monthly Meeting sometime past for Jesse and Bartis Comegys but they have not appeared and the meeting plans to return the certificates.

30/4/1772. A certificate was produced for John George and his wife Rachel and the children: Joseph, Rachel, James, John, Sarah, Thomas and Mary, directed to the monthly meeting in Kent Co. on Delaware.

30/4/1772. John Edmondson produced a few lines from Duck Creek Monthly Meeting, showing him clear of marriage engagements.

30/4/1772. Robert Register by a Friend requested a certificate of removal, to be directed to Duck Creek Monthly Meeting.

30/4/1772. Joseph Berry replaces Wm. Edmondson as clerk. [The record book is about full.]

28/5/1772. Women Friends produced a testimony against Sarah and Lydia Rumbly formerly Register.

28/5/1772. John Dickinson and Lydia Powell declared their intentions of marriage. [They m. 27/6/1772.]

25/6/1772. Women Friends produced certificates of removal for Rachel Edmondson, wife of Francis, and Esther Edmondson, wife of John, to be directed to the monthly meeting of Kent Co. on Delaware.

30/7/1772. Daniel Willson replaces Benjamin Berry as Collector.

30/7/1772. Hannah Turner by a Friends requests leave to take measures the law directs to recover some debts due from persons not of our Society.

30/7/1772. Aaron Atkinson requests leave to take measures the law directs to recover the right of a person not of our Society.

30/7/1772. Daniel Willson replaces Joseph Berry in the care and oversight of Tuckahoe Meeting.

27/8/1772. Queen Anns Meeting offers that Rachel Coventon has been indisposed and her children have neglected attending meetings for some years.

27/8/1772. John Dickinson by a Friend requested a certificate for himself and wife, to be directed to the monthly meeting in Kent Co. on Delaware. 24/9/1772. Women Friends produced a testimony against Mary Cook late

Farebank.

24/10/1772. Women Friends produced a certificate for Priscilla Neal, to be directed to Duck Creek Monthly Meeting.

24/10/1772. John Register requested liberty to defend himself in a suit and to take measures as the law allows in recovering debts due him.

24/10/1772. Thomas Wickersham having removed and settled in these parts, produced a certificate from the monthly meeting of Philadelphia signifying that his conduct had been in good degree orderly, a frequenter of meetings of worship and clear of debts and marriage engagements.

26/11/1772. Solomon Edmondson was received into membership.

26/11/1772. John Berry intends to Wilmington on business, to stay for some time.

31/12/1772. Benjamin Berry is appointed to replace James Kemp in the care and oversight of Tuckahoe Meeting.

25/1/1773. Benjamin Pervin [Parvin] having removed and settled within the verge of this monthly meeting, produced a certificate from the Wilmington Monthly Meeting for himself and wife Sarah, and their daughter Mary.

25/1/1773. Wm. Troth requests a certificate for his son William who is put an apprentice in Philadelphia.

25/2/1773. James Register has been guilty of neglecting our meetings for a long time and guilty of quarreling and fighting.

25/2/1773. Choptank Meeting reports that Isaac Cox has accomplished his marriage by the assistance of a hireling priest.

25/2/1772. Howell Powell is appointed treasurer of this meeting in place of Isaac Cox.

25/3/1772. Women Friends produced a testimony against Elizabeth Hurst late Webb.

25/3/1772. Solomon Edmondson having removed and settled within the verge of Duck Creek Monthly Meeting, persons are appointed to prepare a certificate for him, his wife and children. On 27/4/1773 it is reported that some obstructions have been found. The minutes of 30/9/1773 reveal that there is a dispute between Solomon Edmondson and the executors of the estate of Francis Neal. On

24/2/1774 it was revealed that he had sold a Negro as a slave. On 31/3/1774 he was disowned.

27/4/1773. John Bowers of Kent Co. on Delaware and Mary Ann Powell declare their intentions of marriage. [They m. 29/5/1773.]

24/6/1773. Women Friends produced testimonies against Sarah Mason late Turner and Rachel Richardson late Coventon for their outgoing in marriages.

24/6/1773. Benjamin Parvin requested leave to defend himself in a law suit.

24/6/1773. Aaron Atkinson requested leave to take the measures the law directs to recover a debt due him.

27/7/1773. It appears that Rachel Richardson had a child too soon after marriage.

27/7/1773. Women Friends produced a certificate for Mary Ann Bowers, directed to Duck Creek Monthly Meeting.

26/8/1773. James Berry replaces Joseph Berry as clerk of this meeting.

28/.10/1773. John Berry who lately resided for a time in Wilmington, produced a copy of a minute signifying that he sometimes attended their meetings and has settled his affairs to their satisfaction.

25/11/1773. James Edmondson of Dorchester County and Martha Bartlet declared their intentions to marry. [They m. 31/12/1773.]

25/11/1773. Manumissions and certificates by William Bromwell who now resides in Philadelphia were produced for the freedom of two Negroes, to witt, Lewis and Sam.

30/12/1773. Mary Lightfoot having resided in these parts for sometime, a certificate was produced from Burlington Monthly Meeting.

24/2/1774. Howel Powel informed the meeting that the indisposition of his wife prevented his attending the Quarterly Meeting.

24/2/1774. Women Friends produced a testimony against Sophia Register.

24/2/1774. Joseph Berry was appointed to the oversight of Tuckaho Meeting in place of Benjamin Berry.

28/4/1774. Women Friends produced a certificate of removal for Susanna Edmondson, wife of Solomon Edmondson, and her three children, to wit, Samuel, Mary and Solomon Edmondson, directed to Duck Creek Monthly Meeting.

28/4/1774. The testimony against Sophia Edmondson [Register?] has been presented to her.

28/4/1774. Aron Atkinson requested certificates of removal for three of the children of Obadiah Atkinson, now deceased, to wit, Obadiah, Solomon and Elizabeth, who are placed in Philadelphia.

26/5/1774. James Wainwright is no longer to be considered for membership, he having married by a priest.

26/5/1774. Daniel Richardson and Rebecca Dickinson declared their intentions of marriage. On 26/6/1774 he produced a certificate from Duck Creek Monthly Meeting signifying his clearness in respect to marriage engagements. [They m. 1/7/1774.]

26/6/1774. John Dixon requested leave in a legal manner to recover some debts due him.

20/6/1774. Samuel Register condemned his disorderly conduct.

28/7/1774. John Bartlett replaces Daniel Dickinson as Collector for Third Haven Meeting.

25/8/1774. Women Friends produced a certificate of removal for Rebecca Richardson, wife of Daniel Richardson, directed to Deer Creek Monthly Meeting.

29/9/1774. Joseph Bartlett informs this meeting that he intends to travel to London on business and requests the concurrence of Friends, he being a young man whose conduct has been in a good degree orderly, a frequenter of our religious meetings; the meeting desires his preservation and safe return.

27/10/1774. Park Webb is disowned, he having accomplished his marriage by a hireling priest.

27/10/1774. David Register having removed and settled within the verge of Duck Creek Monthly Meeting, by a Friend requests a certificate.

24/11/1774. Women Friends produced a testimony against Mary Bullen late Lightfoot.

29/12/1774. James Kemp, Jun., having accomplished his marriage by the assistance of a hireling priest, is disowned.

29/12/1774. William Edmondson replaces James Berry as clerk to this meeting.

26/1/1775. Aaron Atkinson produced a manumission for a Negro woman named

Judah.

23/2/1775. Thomas Wickersham requests leave to take measures the law directs to recover a debt.

3/30/1775. Daniel Dickinson has got married to a person not of our Society by the assistance of a Justice of the Peace.

3/30/1775 Women Friends produced testimonies against Elizabeth Rice late Clark, Sarah Cooper late Kemp, and Elizabeth Wainwright late Berry.

3/30/1775 Benjamin Parvin is appointed to keep the register in place of Daniel Dickinson.

27/4/1775. Howel Powel produced manumissions for three Negroes: Richard, Adam and Isaac.

27/4/1775. John Berry applied for a certificate signifying clearness in regard to marriage engagements, to be directed to Cecil Monthly Meeting.

25/5/1775. Testimonies against Rachel Kemp late Harwood, Elizabeth Eaton late Hopkins, and Rachel Sangston late Hopkins.

29/6/1775. Sarah Berry by a Friend requests leave to recover some debts due her.

29/6/1775. Thomas Wilson requests leave to recover a debt.

31/8/1775. Third Haven Meeting reports that William Edmondson complains that Henry Troth in indebted to him and neglects to pay.

31/8/1775. Samuel Register and Ann Wilson declared their intentions to marry. [They m. at Tuckahoe Meeting House on 2/10/1775.]

26/10/1775. James Edmondson complains that Thomas Edmondson is indebted to him and neglects to pay. On 30/11/1775 Thomas Edmondson requested a certificate of removal for himself, wife Sophia and six children: John, Edward, Thomas, Elizabeth, Sophia and Margaret Edmondson, to be directed to Duck Creek Monthly Meeting - certificate delayed awaiting settlement between Thomas Edmndson and James Edmondson. On 25/1/1776 it was reported that Thomas Edmondson hath given security to James Edmondson for what he is indebted to him, and James claims that some repairs ought to be done on the plantation where Thomas lately resided and it is considered that Thomas ought not to be burthened with of the said repairs. A certificate of removal will be forwarded.

28/12/1775. Samuel Rowland and Hannah Turner declared their intentions to marry. [Samuel Rowland of Sussex Co., DE, and Hannah Turner of Caroline Co., m. at Queen Annes Meeting House in Caroline Co. on 30/1/1776.] On 31/7/1777 Hannah Rowland by a friend requested a certificate of removal for three of her children, namely, Hannah, Joseph and John Turner, to be directed to Duck Creek Monthly Meeting. On 29/10/1778 it was reported that certificates of removal heretofore made out for the Hannah, John and Joseph Turner, children of Isaac Turner, dec'd., and Hannah his wife, have miscarried. On 26/11/1778 a letter was prepared to Duck Creek Monthly Meeting confirming the membership of Hannah, John and Joseph Turner and referring to their brother Isaac Turner who had been placed as an apprentice in the compass of Duck Creek Monthly Meeting.

28/12/1775. Women Friends produced a testimony against Rebecca Oxenham late Clark for her outgoing in marriage.

28/12/1775. John Dixon produced to the meeting manumissions and certificates for the freedom of five Negroes: Ben, Lucy, Hannah, Ned and Rose.

28/12/1775. James Berry informs that he expects to proceed in marriage with Mary Bonsall, a member of Wilmington Monthly Meeting and requests a certificate.

25/1/1776. A few lines were received from Cecil Monthly Meeting on behalf of Margaret Berry, wife of John Berry

29/2/1776. Women Friends produced a certificate of removal for Sarah Edmondson, daughter of Peter and Sophia Edmondson, directed to Duck Creek Monthly Meeting.

28/3/1776. Thomas Wickersham and Ann Bartlett declared their intentions of marriage. On 25/4/1776 Thomas produced a certificate from his parents signifying their consent.[Thomas Wickersham, son of Isaac Wickersham of Reading in Berks Co., PA, and Ann Bartlett, daughter of Joseph Bartlett, late of Talbot Co., m. at Third Haven Meeting House, 27/4/1776.]

28/3/1776. James Berry requested to be released of oversight of Samuel Register, he having lately removed within the compass of Tuckahoe Meeting. Henry Sherwood is appointed and Isaac Dixon continues in that service.

25/4/1776. Joseph Kemp, having got joined in marriage with the assistance of a hireling priest with someone not in profession with us, is disowned.

30/5/1776. Mary Berry, wife of James Berry, produced a certificate from Wilmington Monthly Meeting.

27/6/1776. Women Friends inform that Sarah Roberts late Jenkinson has accomplished her marriage by the assistance of a hireling priest; she is disowned.

27/6/1776. A certificate of removal was presented for Hannah Rowland, wife of Samuel Rowland, but further inquiry is apprehended. On 29/8/1776 a certificate is prepared which cites her sober life and conversation; she is a frequenter of meetings for worship and has settled her outward affairs except for slave keeping.

25/7/1776. Southy Wilson does not appear to be in a capacity to make satisfaction for his disorders.

29/8/1776. Women Friends inform that Hannah Register has been guilty of fornication which appears by her having an illegitimate child. She does not appear in a capacity to make satisfaction. She is disowned.

29/8/1776. Women Friends inform that Sarah Rice late Wilson has accomplished her marriage by a hireling priest. She is disowned.

26/9/1776. As to the recommendation of Cathrine Lightfoot as a minister, another month will be left for further consideration. On 2/1/1777 it was decided to recommend her to the Quarterly Meeting.

26/9/1776. Solomon Charles to be received into membership.

26/9/1776. William Edmondson is replaced as clerk by Aron Atkinson.

31/10/1776. William Troth, son of Henry, having removed sometime past from Philadelphia and settled within the compass of this meeting, a certificate has been received.

31/10/1776. Thomas Wickersham produced an account of a wheat faner taken in execution from him valued at £3 for a fine of 40 shillings laid on him for refusing to bear arms or train in the militia, taken by David McIntosh, Collector.

31/10/1776. John Register produced an account of one milch cow taken from him valued at £3.10 for a fine of 40 shillings laid on him for refusing to bear arms or train in the militia, taken by David McIntosh, Collector.

2/1/1777. Elizabeth Ozburn produced a certificate of removal from Philadelphia Monthly Meeting recommending her and her children: Sarah, Lysdia, Elizabeth, Ann and Susanna; also Elizabeth Atkinson, an apprentice.

2/1/1777. Solomon Dawson of Kent Co. and Lydia Bartlett declared their intentions of marriage. He later presented a certificate from Cecil Monthly

Meeting and consent of his parents. [Solomon Dawson, son of Benjamin Dawson of Duck Creek in Kent Co., DE, and Lydia Bartlett, daughter of Joseph Bartlett, late of Talbot Co., m. 1/2/177 at Third Haven Meeting House.]

2/1/1777. John Register produced manumissions for 5 Negroes (unnamed) which were read and recorded.

27/2/1777. Thomas Wilson produced manumissions for 6 Negroes.

27/3/1777. Lydia Dawson, wife of Solomon Dawson, having removed to reside within the compass of Cecil Monthly Meeting, requests a certificate.

27/3/1777. Henry Troth produced a manumission for two Negroes.

24/4/1777. Richard Milton by a Friend requested a certificate of removal to Cecil Monthly Meeting.

29/5/1777. Isaac Dawson requests to defend himself in action of law.

29/5/1777. Women Friends inform that Sarah Charles, wife of Solomon Charles, hath applied to be received into membership.

31/7/1777. Thomas Wilson has suffered considerably by fire. Collections will be made.

25/9/1777. John Bartlett produced an account of one feather bed taken from him valued at £3 for refusing to serve in the militia.

25/9/1777. Howel Powel produced an account of one cow and calf valued at £5 for a demand for refusing to serve in the militia.

27/11/1777. Manumissions were received from Samuel and Hannah Rowland for 2 Negroes; from Sarah Register for two; from Magdalen Kemp for two; from John Kemp for two; from Samuel Harwood Senr. for five, from Samuel Register for three; from James Turner for one - all which were placed in the hands of James Berry to be recorded.

27/11/1777. Samuel Troth produced a certificate of removal from Wilmington Monthly Meeting signifying Friends' Unity and clearness with respect to marriage.

27/11/1777. Isaac Dixon being removed by death, John Bartlett is appointed to replace him to have the oversight of Thirdhaven Meeting with James Berry.

25/12/1777. A certificate of removal for Rebecca Smith was received from Cecil Monthly Meeting.

29/1/1778. Isaac Dixon being removed by death John Register is appointed in his place with James Berry to have the care of Bayside Meeting.

29/1/1778. Women Friends inform that Lydia Gary late Clark and Mary Sangston late Morgan have have got their marriages accomplished contrary to the good order used amongst Friends. They are disowned.

29/1/1778. Aaron Atkinson is replaced as clerk by John Register.

26/3/1778. Manumissions were received from the following Friends: John Jenkinson for two Negroes; Elizabeth Powel for four; Daniel Wilson for two; Solomon Neal for one.

28/5/1778. James Edmondson produced an account of his sufferings for refusing to train in the militia.

28/5/1778. Persons were appointed to make inquiry and to prepare a certificate respecting Sarah Berry and her daughter Mary, directed to Duck Creek Monthly Meeting.

25/6/1778. Aaron Parratt does not appear to be in a disposition to comply with the direction of the Yearly Meeting in regard to slave keeping; also charged with drinking to excess and having taken an affirmation which we apprehend enjoins him to contribute to the war. On 26/11/1778 a testimony against Aaron Parratt was published disowning him and stating he had received slaves from his late father in law Francis Neale's estate but failed to restore them to their natural state of liberty. He has been disguised with spiritous liquor and taken an affirmation to support War.

25/6/1778. Richard Milton having returned to reside within the compass of this monthly meeting produced a certificate from Cecil Monthly Meeting; has settled his affairs and is clear of marriage engagements.

25/6/1778. Cathrine Lightfoot has requested a certificate to Duck Creek Monthly Meeting.

25/6/1778. Samuel Register is disowned, having neglected attending religious meetings and having taken an affirmation which we apprehend enjoins him to support War for which purpose he hath contributed towards hiring a substitute in leave of personal service.

27/8/1778. James Edmondson requests to take leave to take legal methods with a persons who has trespassed upon him.

24/9/1778. Sarah Register requests a certificate to be directed to Duck Creek Monthly Meeting. On 29/10/1778 a certificate was prepared showing her conduct was in a good degree orderly, a frequenter of religious meetings, and clear of marriage engagements.

29/10/1778. By the report of the Committee appointed to visit those who hold slaves it appears that Peter Webb is possessed of divers of that people whom he holds in a state of slavery, both of those over and under age. On 25/2/1779 he was disowned.

31/12/1778. Thomas Wilson replaces John Bartlett as Collector for Third Haven Meeting.

28/1/1779. Third Haven offers that John Berry for sometime has neglected attending meetings, has been guilty of gaming, has been keeping undue company, and taken an affirmation which we apprehend enjoins him to support War.

28/1/1779. John Bartlet and Richard Bartlet produced accounts of their sufferings for muster fines and taxes laid to support war.

28/1/1779. Isaac Gilpin produced a certificate from Concord Monthly Meeting signifying his birth right among Friends, his clearness of marriage engagements and that he had settled his outward affairs.

28/1/1779. John Register produced a manumission for one Negro.

25/2/1779. John Hopkins produced a manumission for one Negro.

25/3/1779. A certificate of removal was received for Hannah Osborn from the monthly meeting of Philadelphia.

25/3/1779. The children of Solomon Charles are to be received into membership.

25/3/1779. John Register produced an account of his sufferings

25/3/1779. John Register is replaced as clerk by Richard Bartlet.

29/4/1779. Henry Troth requests a certificate of removal for his son John who is placed an apprentice to a Friends in New Garden Monthly Meeting.

29/4/1779. Bernard Gilpin, an apprentice, produced a certificate from Concord Monthly Meeting [PA].

29/4/1779. A request was made for a certificate of removal for Elizabeth Osborn and her children, Hannah, Sarah, Lydia, Elizabeth, Ann and Susanna; also for

Elizabeth Atkinson - to be directed to the monthly meeting of Wilmington.

29/4/1779. Robert Dixon apprehends the necessity of a voyage to endeavour the recovery of his health and requests a certificate.

27/5/1779. Mary Ann Parrat does not appear disposed to release her slaves.

27/5/1779. From Third Haven Meeting: Thomas Harwood has accomplished his marriage with the assistance of a priest. Disowned.

27/5/1779. From Choptank: Meeting: Thomas Welch requests to be taken under the notice of Friends. He was received into membership on 29/7/1779.

27/5/1779. Thomas Wickersham produced an account of his sufferings for refusing the paying of a tax to support the War.

24/6/1779. James Wainwright is received into membership along with his sons John and James.

24/6/1779. Solomon Neal produced an account of his sufferings for refusing to pay the tax to support the War.

24/6/1779. Mary Harwood, formerly Harwood, has accomplished her marriage with the assistance of a priest. Disowned.

29/7/1779. Elizabeth Wainwright condemns her outgoing in marriage.

29/7/1779. Samuel Troth requested a certificate of removal to Cecil Monthly Meeting.

29/7/1779. Joseph Berry produced an account of his sufferings on account for refusing to pay a tax to support the War.

26/8/1779. A certificate received from Duck Creek Monthly Meeting for Edward Cox and Sarah Cox, children of Powel Cox, they being in their minority.

26/8/1779. William Edmondson who keeps the book to record manumission of slaves is replaced by Richard Bartlet

28/10/1779. Tristram Needles and Anna Buckbee declared their intentions of marriage. [Tristram Needles and Ann Buckbee, both of Talbot co., m. 1/12/1779 at Choptank Meeting House.]

25/11/1779. Third Haven Meeting: Rebecca Hopkins has neglected attending meetings and has joined another society.

25/11/1779. Robert Dixon having declined his intended voyage to sea, returned his certificate.

30/12/1779. Mary Ann Parratt has manumitted two Negroes and that appears to be all the ones she has in her possession that she had a right to manumit.

CECIL MONTHLY MEETING MINUTES
1698-1779

9/9/1698. William Bayly hath walked disorderly

8/12/1698. David Croly and Mary Everett declared their intentions to marry. {They m. 15/1/1699.]

12/2/1699. Joseph Porter and Shusannah Wethrell declared their intentions to marry. [They m. 10/3/1699.]

14/4/1699. Henry Hosier and James Barber to see that Reachell Biggers (Boyers?) receives her estate that her father left her.

12/5/1699. A report that Mathew (Matheis?) Pope had been in drink and fighting with a man.

9/6/1699. John Toas and Joyce Quinney declared their intentions to marry. [They m. 14/7/1699.]

... [very faint - unable to read]...

8/5/1702. Wm. Mofett was given a certificate signifying his clearness in relation to marriage in these parts.

8/5/1702. John Bersens condemns his taking a wife out of good order.

12/6/1702. A concern about the orphans of Sutton Queny. A visit will be made to John Toas.

11/9/1702. William Welch and Denneabel Barker declared their intentions to marry. [They m. 3/12/1702.]

10/1/1703. Mary Pope desires to proceed in matters of her husband's estate.

9/4/1703. Shusannah Porter desires advice of this meeting what she had best to doe in matters relating to her husband's estate.

-/9/1703. William Trew and Martha Pope declared their intentions to marry. [They m. 15/10/1703.]

-/3/1704. John Gumly and Deborah Barber declared their intentions to marry. [They m. 29/4/1704.]

11/8/1704. Aquilla Johns of Calvert Co. and Mary Hosier of Kent Co., declared their intentions to marry. Acquilla produced a certificate from the monthly meeting at West River. [They m. 16/9/1704.]

9/3/1705. A concern was expressed for the orphans of Peter Porter.

11/5/1705. A difference exists between James Barber and Casper Hoodt and

Sarah his wife, James having formerly bought a piece of land of Steaven Coleman the said Sarah's former husband.

12/4/1706. John Lewis desires a certificate from this meeting in order to marry a friend at Salem.

13/9/1706. Visited Elizabeth Hamour(?) and dealt with her going to a priest to be married.

8/11/1706. John Hart desires a certificate on account of marriage with a woman in these parts

10/10/1707. Wm. Thomas and Joanna Hosier declared their intentions to marry. [They m. 22/11/1707.]

9/4/1708. To visit Susannah Williams concerning her outgoing in marriage.

***8/7/1708. Abraham Melton and Mary Wyett declared their intentions to marry.

***8/7/1708. John Ball and Hester Gush declared their intentions to marry.

14/7/1709. Gilbert Faulkner plans to remove to Philadelphia.

14/12/1710. Charity Spearman, widow of James Kelley having contrary to truth taken a husband and also run into several other evils and light actions with the testimony of truth ...

13/11/1711. Mary Pope now Mary Young has taken a husband contrary to the good order of truth.

***13/11/1711. John Pitt and Rebecka Hosier declared their intentions declared their intentions to marry.

9/5/1712. Henry Hosier requests a certificate from this meeting of his clearness of marriage.

13/6/1712. James Barber and Barbarah Kelley declared their intentions to marry.

8/1/1712. Concern for Eliz: Pope now Graves on account of her marrying out.

11/9/1713. George Warner requests a certificate concerning his clearness of marriage.

9/4/1714. To visit Thomas Rasin concerning his disorderly marriage.

9/4/1714. Isaac England (produced a certificate from Duck Creek Monthly Meeting) and Eliz: Hoodt declared their intentions to marry. [They m. 12/6/1714.]

12/1/1713. Friends of Chester Meeting hath given account to this meeting that they have visited Abraham Milton on account of his marriage out of the good order of truth and he has given them a paper condemning his disorderly marriage.

9/9/1715. Morgan Brown requests a certificate signifying his clearness of marriage engagements.

9/11/1716. Samll. Smith and Judith Hoodt declared their intentions to marry. [They m. 2/2/17??]

10/5/1717. James Barber and Phillip Reasin were removed by death, they being overseers.

14/11/1718. Daniel Hoodt having resided sometime within the compass of this monthly meeting but removing to Philadelphia and have intentions of altering his condition in order hereunto, he hath by a friend requested a certificate.

8/4/1720. James Corse Senr. being overseer of Cecil Monthly Meeting, was removed by death.

***10/6/1720. Richard Hays and Mary Dunkin declared their intentions to marry, having parents consent.

***9/3/1722. John Hebron and Eliz: Brues(?) declared their intentions to marry. The monthly meeting finds that they are cohabiting.

*12/7/1722. Daniell Large and Mary Bentley declared their intentions to marry. On 14/9/1722 it was reported that the marriage of Danll. Large and Mary Bently had been orderly accomplished.

10/8/1722. Richard Beevins requests a certificate.

13/12/1722. James Kelley was some months agoe given himself into drunkenness.

11/7/1723. Benja. Kelley accused of loose conversation.

11/7/1723. George Dunkin proposes to visit his antient mother and some meetings in the province of Pennsylvania and requests a certificate.

11/10/1723. Daniell Mullikin has acknowledged his taking liberty in drinking.

12/12/1723. Whereas James Barber according to his last will left his child under the care of Daniell Mullikin but said Daniel dying this meeting has a concern and will visit widow Mullikin.

9/4/1724. John Everett removing himself out of this province to East or West Jersey and being about to alter his condition in relation to marriage, requests a certificate.

8/5/1724. Because John Everett resided sometime in Talbot Co., that meeting is requested to give him a certificate if appropriate.

8/5/1724. George Elliott, Junr. having taken a wife contrary to good order.

9/7/1724. Ed. Allibone is not able to come to our meetings because of old age.

*12/3/1725. James Kelley and Jane Meade declared their intentions to marry. On 14/5/1725 it was reported that the marriage of James Kelley and Jane Meade had been orderly accomplished.

8/7/1725. Joseph Warner requests a certificate on account of marriage.

8/10/1725. Jno. Corse requests a certificate to signify his clearness of marriage to be directed to Friends of Duck Creek Meeting in New Castle Co.

9/9/1726. Papers are to be drawn up to condemn Benjamin Kellee's unchristian like practices.

*9/9/1726. Thomas Thompson of Talbot Co. and Rachel George declared their intentions to marry. On 11/11/1726 it was reported that the marriage of Thomas Thompson and Rachel George had been accomplished.

*8/1/1727. Stephen Hoskins of Chester Co. (Meeting at Providence), Pennsylvania, and Sarah Warner declared their intentions to marry. On 10/3/1727 it was reported that the marriage of Stephen Hoskins had been orderly accomplished.

9/6/1727. Robt. George, Junr. condemns his disorderly marriage.

11/8/1727. William Corse was condemned for publick scandal by being proved guilty of fornication with a certain Alice Brown.

10/11/1727. Thomas Garrett produced a certificate from the monthly meeting at New Garden dated 25/12/1726.

8/11/1728. James Tibbetts having by his last Will left his children in the care of this monthly meeting.

12/1/1729. Whereas William Spearman late dec'd. left his son Francis Spearman under the care of our monthly meeting - to be bound to the trade of carpenter and joiner.

11/4/1729. A committee is to appear at court in order to prevent Thomas Maslin's children from being taken from among Friends. [The son named Thomas Maslin chose Thomas Rasin as his guardian but the court kept the other children as being too young to choose a guardian.]

13/6/1729. Joseph Georg requests a certificate respecting affairs of marriage to be directed to the monthly meeting in Talbot Co.

10/7/1729. Thomas Garnet produced a certificate on behalf of his brother Jonathan Garnet and his wife Mary, from New Garden Monthly Meeting dated 26/2/1729. A committee was appointed to let [lease] the mill which belonged to James Tibbet.

5/8/1729. A committee was appointed to visit James Course and his wife to enquire whether or not they were accessory in the disorderly marriage of their daughter with a man not of our Society.

10/10/1729. A difference exists between Henry Trulock and Georg Dunkan concerning a sheep.

11/12/1729. A paper concerning Samuel Smith's affair will be sent to Duck Creek Monthly Meeting.

11/12/1729. Joseph Warner advised this meeting to prevent Stephen Hopkins from removing his brother George Warner's children out of this province. The meeting agrees to allow the children to go if Stephen Hopkins gives security that they will be given sufficient education and will not be bound out.

8/2/1730. Gilbert Falconar produced a certificate from Kennett Monthly Meeting in Pennsylvania dated 7/1/1729/30; the reason for such a delay after he had settled was that his wife wanted to be joined to Duck Creek Meeting and he intended here.

8/2/1730. Stephen Hoskins by a friend has requested a certificate but inasmuch as he has gone out of the Province without making up his account with the Commissary General for the estate of Georg Warner, dec'd., the opinion of the meeting is not to recommend him.

14/8/1730. Thomas Maslin is bound to Michael Corse to learn the trade of carpenter and joiner.

10/12/1730. At the death of Joseph Warner, Richard Tibbet an orphan of James Tibbet, is removed to Jno. Ball's care.

8/7/1731. Tibbet's mill soon after Jno. Gail took possession was totally ruined by extreme weather; the monthly meeting proposes to allow him one month's rent for rebuilding the house and mill.

8/1/1732. Ann Warner is in danger (as she thinks) of being damaged in her estate by Stephen Hoskins going out ot the province and neglecting to account with the commissary for Georg Warner's estate, her dec'd. husband.

14/4/1732. Samuel Tibbett, orphan of James Tibbett, is to be bound to William Trew to learn the trade of carpenter, boatwright or sawyer. On 14/12/1738. Samuel Tibbitt, orphan of James Tibbitt, complained that William Trew, his master, was short in complying with his part of the indenture in neglecting to teach him a trade according to the tenour of said indenture. On 14/1/1739. William Trew and Samuel Tibbit being present, it was agreed that William Trew shall let Thos. Maslin have the said Samuel upon tryal for a trade until next monthly meeting. On 11/2/1739 it was William Trew signed over Samuel Tibbit to Thomas Maslin. James Corse and Michael Corse, appointed overseers.

13/7/1732. Morgan Brown was disowned because of his excessive drinking and quarreling.

13/7/1732. Thomas Garnett acknowledges his excessive drinking.

14/1/1733. Thomas Garnett has died; his Will is to be inspected to see if he left some of his children under the care of Friends.

11/2/1733. John Gail being (by ill circumstances) obliged to depart this province left Tibbitt's mill under the care of Tobe Thomas who refuses to pay any part of the income of the said mill unless the monthly meeting will defend him from any demands of John Gaile to which the Monthly Meeting agrees.

*11/5/1733. David Thomas and Ann Warner declared their intentions to marry. On 12/7/1733 it was reported that the marriage of David Thomas and Ann Warner had been orderly accomplished.

12/7/1733. George Dunkan intends to visit his children in Chester Co., Pennsylvania.

12/7/1733. Henry Thomas having an intention of marriage with Elizabeth Troth, daughter of Henry Troth of Talbot Co., dec'd., requests a certificate.

9/8/1733. William Trew and Hannah Bodien declared their intentions to marry. [They m. 28/9/1733.]

14/9/1733. Michael Corse having an intention of marriage with Mary England, daughter of Isaac England of Kent Co., Maryland, dec'd., and now belonging to a monthly meeting in Kent Co., Pennsylvania [DE], requests a certificate.

12/10/1733. The Friends appointed to appear at Duck Creek Monthly Meeting to complain against Daniel Corbitt alias Cormick reports that they having had an opportunity with him before the sitting of the meeting to discourse him about signing the deed of sale he thereupon did agree to sign the said deed if some able friend or friends on behalf of our monthly meeting would give him a sufficient bond to indemnify him in so doing. David Perkins and Francis Lamb report that they have lett or rented the mill called Tibbetts Mill to John Hawkins of our county, carpenter, on the best terms they could gain which terms are as followeth: The said John Hawkins to be put in possession of said mill on the fourteenth day of this instant for the term of one year at the rate or rent of 66 bushels of wheat for the said term of one year to be delivered at Sassafras Ferry on the 14th day of the 10 mo. In the ensuing year 1734 and on the next day following peaceably deliver up and surrender the said mill.

12/10/1733. Henry Hosier at his own request was discharged from his place as overseer.

9/11/1733. [Cecil and Chester meetings represented.] The Friends appointed to get the deed of sale for James Tibbetts' plantation signed - not having complyed are continued to compleat that service. David Perkins produced an obligation for 1400 lbs. of tobacco to this meeting signed by William Pearce to Jobe Thomas and assigned by the said Jobe over to our monthly meeting in part pay of the rent of Tibbetts' mill which obligation is put again into the hands of David Perkins in order to get it paid as soon as may be. David Perkins informs this meeting that he has confirmed the terms on which he rented Tibbetts Mill (in writing) with John Hawkins and hath taken a bond of £40.

13/1/1734. The Friends appointed to settle accounts with Doctor Thomas Williams and Jobe Thomas on behalf of the monthly meeting make a report that there appears due in the said Docktors hands to the meeting the sum of £13 which became due on the 15th day of the 2nd month last past; £11.8.5 whereof this meeting has given John(?) Pratt an order for and the remaining part being one £1.11.7 is hereby ordered to Abraham Milton. And from Jobe Thomas there appears due to the meeting £8.10.2; 24 shillings whereof is ordered to David Perkins for which they are to account when received. The several orders being for charges out, upon James Tibbetts' orphans.

8/3/1734. Francis Spareman and Jannet Corse declared their intentions of marriage. [They m. 17/4/1734.]

12.4/1734. William Collins being present was dealt with for disorderly walking. Richard Johns produced a certificate on behalf of himself and wife from fhe monthly meeting at West River bearing date 23rd of 9th month 1733.

10/5/1734. It was decided to endeavor to take under the care of friends Thomas Garnett's son Jonathan.

11/7/1734. Edward Beck of Chester Meeting having sometime ago been guilty of drinking to excess was dealt with in this meeting and he condemned his excess to the satisfaction of Friends.

8/8/1734. Reference to Jonathan Garnett's bro. George.

11/10/1734. Edward Comegys at his own request was discharged form his office as clerk and Thomas Bowers appointed in his stead.

8/11/1734. George Dunkan appraised this meeting of the outgoing of his son Wm. Dunkan in marriage despite his being advised to the contrary.

12/12/1734. Tibbets Mill rented out to James Stout for £11 per year.

12/12/1734. William Dunkan, son of George and Mary Dunkan, is disowned for marrying out. Received of Thomas Williams a sum of £3.15.0 being part of the rent due for Tibbets plantation.

12/12/1734. John Ball having an intention of marriage with Jane Turner of Talbot Co., requests a certificate.

14/3/1735. There is dissatisfaction with Wm. Collins of the method he took in picking up the condemnation of his disorder. Friends expect him to affix the condemnation of his disorder up at the most publick door of the court house at the next court and on the second day of court. [which he failed to do.]

11/7/1735. William Collins' letter of condemnation: Whereas the subscriber (being one reputed a Quaker) some considerable time past in the town of Chester unhappily (by drinking to excess) became incapable of commanding my own behaviour thereby disturbing and discomposing myself and others (the Court not excepted) for which I am truly concerned, and hope that my future behaviour together with the costs(?)my attone for my offences desiring all who may be forward in reflections to point at me alone excluding the Society of which I was deemed a member untill my disorder whereby I became disunited until a Christian decorum shall — my admission. Signed by Willm. Collins.

6/8/1735. Joseph Bartlet and Martha Milton declared intentions of marriage, Joseph living in the verge of another monthly meeting. is required to produce a certificate declaring his life and conversation and clearness of all others on account of marriage and consent of his parents before any proceeding be made herein before the next monthly meeting. [They m. 11/10/1735. at Chester Meeting House.]

6/8/1735. Jno. Roe and Jane Eubanks declare their intentions of marriage. [They m. 13/10/1735.]

6/8/1735. Thomas Maslin and Mary Ann Lamb declare their intentions of marriage. [They m. 11/10/1735.]

10/10/1735. George Dunkan Junr. and Margret Kinsey declared their intentions of marriage. [They m. 21/11/1735.]

10/10/1735. George Duncak applies for a certificate on the account of Steven Hoskins who is moved out of these part into Pennsylvania.

14/11/1735. The mill has been rented to James Robass.

11/12/1735. A certificate for Stephen Hoskins will not be granted until he has accounted for a disorder committed by him.

11/12/1735. Reported that Elizabeth, the daughter of James Corse having acknowledged a man not of our Society to be her husband, and that the said James by some circumstances — had not carried himself so clear in that affair as becomes one possessing the Truth.

11/12/1735. It was reported that Francis Lamb sometime ago did at a funeral outwardly conform with those who differ in persuasion from us by going into their worship house and there remaining uncovered during the time of performing their service and that the said Francis since then has had one of his daughters married to a man not of our society by and with the consent of him the said Francis. On 11/6/1736 Francis Lamb's produced a letter condemning his behaviour at a service of the Church of England.

12/3/1736. Ann Thomas accounts well this meeting for the board, cloathing and schooling of Richard Tibbet. John Ball receives from this meeting £--- due to him for boarding and cloathing of Richard Tibbet.

.

12/11/1736. Joseph Dunkan, about to remove from hence into Pennsylvania, requested a certificate.

9/12/1736. John Phillips some time ago was accidently disordered with strong liquor. On 9/1/1737 he produced the following letter - Whereas it hath so happened on the 22nd day of 10th mo. last past that being at Hero Town, where I unnecessarily (not considering the then present state of my body, and being greatly overcome with the rigors of the season by riding to Town on that day did indulge my self in drink — found it produced other effects; for upon the road going home to my no small surprise I found the strength thereof prevailed so far upon the weakness of my constitution at that time that I was greatly disordered thereby and the same became not only a trouble to myself but maybe obvious to others and being a ... ?

9/12/1736. Richard Tibbet, one of the orphans of James Tibbet being removed ... last third month from Wm. Thomas to Abraham Milton and from thence to David Hulle(?) George Dunkan having made some — to this meeting concerning the said orphan, the meeting has thought fit (with David's consent) to remove him to George Dunkan's till next monthly meeting.

13./5/1737.James Claypool applies to this meeting for a few lines of recommendation to Friends in Philadelphia on account of marriage, which was granted.

14/7/1737. George Dunkan Junr condemns his disorder.

4/8/1737. Thomas Richardson and Ann Thomas announced intentions of marriage. [They m. 10/9/1737.]

9/9/1737. Edward Comegys and Mary Thrawl announced their intentions of marriage. [They m. 15/10/1737.]

14/10/1737. George Dunkan condemns his having carnal knowledge before marriage of the body of the woman he has since married.

14/4/1738. George Read at his own request is discharged from all those affairs he has been intrusted with by the monthly meeting. George Dunkan at his own request is discharged from being overseer of the widdows and orphans belonging to Cecil Monthly Meeting. Thomas Bowers at his own request was discharged from being overseer for the state of Cecil Meeting and from being overseer of the ministers of Cecil Meeting.

14/4/1738. George Dunkan is asked to ask his son George Dunkan reasons for his declining coming to meetings.

14/4/1738. The reasons given by Jno. Phillips to this meeting for his declining coming to our meetings of worship was not satisfactory. On ?/9/1738 it was recorded that John Phillips being dead puts an end to all further proceedings on his account.

?/9/1738. A certificate was prepared for Richard Johns. George Read having sometime ago been overtaken liquor it is the sense of the meeting that he should prepare a letter of condemnation [which he presented at the next meeting].

?/10/1738. David Hull having in intention of going into Pennsylvania and visiting some meetings requests a certificate.

?/11/1738. Thomas Bowers resigns as clerk.

14/12/1738. Henry Covinton and Rachel Roe of Queen Anns County announced intentions of marriage. [They m. 19/4/1738.]

14/12/1738. Isaac Milton having an intention of marriage with Ann Bartlett, daughter of James Bartlett within the verge of the monthly meeting in Talbot Co. made application to this meeting for a certificate respecting that affair.

14/12/1738. Daniel Hull having an intention of moving out of the verge of our monthly meeting made application to this meeting for a certificate recommending him to the meeting in Kent County upon Delaware.

11/2/1739. William Thomas has taken to wife the daughter of a friend in Talbot Co. in a disorderly manner in going to the priest for marriage.

*7/3/1739. Howel Buckingham and Barbara Corse declared their intentions of marriage. Howel being a member of another monthly meeting must produce a certificate showing his clearness of all other women on account of marriage. On 11/5/1739 it was reported that the marriage of Howel Buckingham had been accomplished in good order.

***7/3/1739. Howel Powel Junr. of Talbot Co. and Ann Elisabeth Bodien declared their intentions of marriage; Howel is to produce a certificate.

13/4/1739. Sasafrax Meeting established on Swan Creek as within the verge of Cecil Monthly Meeting; John Browning and Joshua Vanzant are appointed overseers of the meeting.

12/7/1739. Griffith Thomas of New Castle Co., Pennsylvania [DE], and Alis Browne declared their intentions of marriage. [They m. 9/8/1739.]

14/9/1739. John Brown being threatened to be compelled to bear military arms at muster, made application to this meeting for a certificate signifying he is in unity with us which was granted and directed to Capt. Christopher Bateman.

14/3/1740. A certificate importing the life and conversations of Joseph England and also his clearness respecting marriage was read with approbation.

11/12/1740. Isaac England and Ann Corse declared their intentions of marriage. [They m. 13/1/1741.]

13/3/1741. James Claypole has taken a wife not of the Society and married by a priest.

12/6/1741. Samuel Tibbett being arrived at age applies to have the Will of his father delivered to him. On 13/11/1741 Samuel Tibbett informed the meeting that he has come to an agreement with James Robass about the mill and therefore discharged the meeting of that affair.

12/6/1741. Michael Corse desires to be discharged as overseer of Cecil Meeting which is granted.

5/8/1741. Thomas Richardson and Thomas Bowers to be overseers of Cecil Meeting.

10/1/1742. Enquiries to be made in response to Joseph England's application for a certificate on account of marriage.

10/1/1742. Henry Brooks having given security to the county for the maintenance of a base born child, therefore this meeting expects him to appear at the next meeting. On 13/7/1749 Henry Brooks was disowned.

10/1/1742. Francis Lamb Junr having gone out in marriage, this meeting expects him to condemn his outgoing.

12/3/1742. Thomas Bowers and Thomas Richardson resigned their places as overseers of Cecil Meeting.

10/9/1742. Michael Corse and Thomas Bowers were appointed as overseers of the ministry in Cecil meeting and William Trew and Joseph George for Chester

Meeting and Joshua Vansant and John Welch for Sassafras meeting.

*9/12/1742. David Perkins and Rebeckah Taylor declared their intentions of marriage. On 11/3/1743 it was reported that the marriage of David Perkins and Rebeckah Taylor was accomplished in good order.

9/1/1743. Bartholomew Garnett produced a certificate from the monthly meeting at New Garden in Pennsylvania.

11/3/1743. Michael Offley and Phebe Corse declared their intentions of marriage; Michael belonging to the monthly meeting at Duck Creek. [They m. 8/4/1743.]

13/5/1743. David Hall and Samuel Wallis were appointed to give an account of the widows and orphans belonging to Cecil Meeting.

14/10/1743. It was mentioned by a Friend that there is a difference subsisting between John Corse and Francis Lamb about land affairs and have chosen George Dunkan, David Hull, Thomas Bowers, Thomas Richardson, Joshua Vansant, Jacob Caulk, and James Claypool to decide the said difference between them.

8/12/1743. John Corse at his own request is discharged as overseer of Cecil Meeting. Michael Corse and Thomas Bowers at their requests are discharged from being overseers of the ministry of Cecil Meeting.

11/2/1744. Francis Spareman is expected to condemn his disorderly marriage. On 11/5/1744 he submitted his letter of condemnation.

9/3/1744. James Corse Junr. having gone out by a disorderly marriage is expected to condemn his disorder and appear at the next monthly meeting. On 11/5/1744 it was reported that James Corse appeared cold and indifferent to those Friends who visited on account of his disorder.

13/4/1744. Joseph Garnett informed this meeting that his brother Bartholomew could not well attend the services hereof and desires that Friends defer his affair till next monthly meeting. On 9/8/1744 Bartholomew Garnett appeared and produced a letter condemning his taking a wife by a priest.

11/5/1744. James Tibbett now of age will receive income from rent of his father's plantation.

8/6/1744. Prince Snow and Mary his wife (lately joyned to Sassafras Meeting) desire to be taken under the care of Friends.

12/7/1744. Samuel Tibbitt produced a letter condemning his going to a priest to be married. On 13/2/1760 it was decided to visit Samuel Tippet to acquaint him to be at our next meeting to give reasons why he does not cohabit with his wife.

On 10/9/1760 Samuel Tippit was disowned.

9/8/1744. Daniel Mifflin and Mary Warner, and Joseph Maxwel and Sarah Warner declared their intentions of marriage. Daniel and Joseph were required to produce certificates on account of marriage and likewise consent of parents and guardians if any there be. [Daniel Mifflin and Mary Warner m. 15/9/1744 and Joseph Maxfield of Worcester Co. and Sarah Warner of Kent Co. m. 14/9/1744.]

14/9/1744. James Corse produced a letter condemning his taking a wife by a priest.

12/10/1744. Jacob Caulk of Sassafras meeting having been repeatedly overtaken in liquor is to be visited.

9/11/1744. George Reason having an intention of marriage with Sarah Powel of Talbot Co. requests a certificate on that account.

13/9/1745. John Gale and Bathsheba Lamb declared their intentions of marriage. On 11/10/1745 it was noted that John Gale's life and conversation from the report has not been in all respects such as Friends would wish; it is hoped that there will be an amendment for the future. They are permitted to accomplish their intentions. On 10/10/1746 John Gale produced his letter condemning his drinking to excess. [They m. 11/10/1745.]

8/11/1745. Philip Milton and Hannah Bodien declared their intentions of marriage. On 12/1/1746 it was reported that Philip Milton has gone from among Friends in a disorderly marriage. On 11/4/1746 it was reported that Philip Milton will not condemn his disorderly marriage.

12/12/1745. Samuel Curry and Mary Corse declared their intentions of marriage. On 12/1/1745/46 Samuel Curry appeared with a certificate of clearness on account of marriage. [They m. 13/1/1745/46.]

12/1/1746. Nathan Wright and Mary Tillotson declared their intentions of marriage. On 9/2/1746 Nathan Wright and Mary Tillotson did not appear. [Mary was indisposed.] [They m. 15/3/1746.]

9/2/1746. Oliver Caulk intending to take a wife out the verge of our monthly meeting requests a certificate respecting that affair.

13/6/1746. Edward Lamb about to remove from within the verge of this monthly meeting desires a certificate for himself and wife to Gunpowder Monthly Meeting.

7/8/1746. Daniel Dickinson of Talbot Co. and Mary Hosier declare their intentions of marriage. On 11/12/1746 it was reported that the marriage of Daniel Dickinson and Mary Hosier had been accomplished in good order.

7/8/1746. Informed that Jacob Caulk continues his immoderate practice of drinking to excess. On 11/1/1747 a letter was presented from Jacob Caulk condemning his disorder of drinking to excess.

12/6/1747. Our Friend Joseph Newby of Narquimons Co. in North Carolina produced a certificate.

9/7/1747. John Barns produced a letter condemning his disorderly marriage.

9/7/1747. James Corse and Susannah Perkins declared their intentions of marriage. On 6/8/1747 it was reported that James Corse having first appeared in our monthly meeting and there declared his intentions of marriage and before the next ensuing meeting went to a priest and accomplished the same.

6/8/1747. William Reason acquainted this meeting with his intention of marriage with a Friend in Virginia and requests a certificate.

11/9/1747. Joseph Dunkan produced a certificate from Abington in Philadelphia for himself and wife.

13/11/1747. A complaint was made that Richard Tibbett has lately been guilty of ... which brings a publick Scandal. On 9/1/1748 it was reported that Richard Tibbett having departed this life all further dealing with him ceases.

13/11/1747. Informed that Writtson Browning has been guilty of disorder in keeping his hat on in time of publick prayer.

13/5/1748. Whereas James Corse, son of James and Ann Corse, having married a woman not of our profession, is disowned.

13/5/1748. James Wyats requests to be taken under the care of Friends.

10/6/1748. Henry Hosier produced a paper condemning his taking a wife contrary to the directions of our discipline.

10/6/1748. Richard Hosier being by the death of his mother and tenour of his father's will and testament fallen under the care of our monthly meeting; this meeting appoints his brother Henry Hosier as his guardian.

10/6/1748. Joseph George and Abraham Milton appointed as overseers of the ministry in Chester Meeting.

14/7/1748. Daniel Hull and Martha Thraul declared their intentions of their marriage. [They m. 5/8/1748.]

5/8/1748. Hannah Falconar having an intention of moving out of this Province made application by Samuel Wallis for a certificate.

9/9/1748. Esau Watkins has broke unity with Friends by taking a wife of different persuation from us and being married by a hireling priest. On 14/4/1749 Esau

Watkins was disowned.

14/10/1748. Benjamin Feris produced a certificate from Friends in Dutchess Co. in the province of New York.

14/10/1748. John Corse requested a certificate for his son who has settled in Kent Co. on Delaware.

11/11/1748. William Trew and Mary George declared their intentions of marriage. [They m. 8/1/1748/9.]

8/1/1749. James Welsh produced a letter condemning his disorderly marriage.

10/3/1749. Thomas Brooke having taken a wife after the manner of those who differ from us in religious principles, is to be acquainted that Friends expect him to condemn his disorder. [He refused.]

12/5/1749. Powel Cox and Mary Hull declared their intentions of marriage, he belonging to another monthly meeting. [They m. 10/6/1749.]

12/5/1749. Thomas Emory and Sarah Bartlet declared their intentions of marriage. [They m. 9/6/1749.]

12/5/1749. Francis Lamb produces a letter condemning his drinking to excess.

12/5/1749. William Rasin having been guilty of some irregularities is expected to condemn same. On 13/10/1749 William Rasin appeared and acknowledged his misconduct to the satisfaction of the meeting.

13/7/1749. Michael Corse having departed this life who had the register of births, burials and marriages belonging to Friends in his hand, the meeting appointed Samuel Wallis to take the said register into his custody.

13/10/1749. Joshua Vansant and Isabela Bowers declared their intentions of marriage. [They m. 11/10/1749.]

14/12/1749. A difference subsists between Henry Brooks and George Rasin.

10/2/1750. Henry Brooks having commenced a suit in law against George Rasin concerning the difference subsisting between them the meeting is desirous to settle the difference in a more amicable manner.

***9/3/1750. John Smith and Mary Milton declared their intentions of marriage.

11/5/1750. Lewis Clothier having been sometime since disguised in liquor and thereby brought dishonour on the Truth he professes this meeting expects him to condemn his disorder. On 13/1/1751 Lewis Clothier condemned his drinking to excess.

11/5/1750. Gershom Mott Junr and Rachel Vansant declared their intentions of marriage, he belonging to another monthly meeting. [They m. 8/6/1750.] On 15/2/1751 Gershom Mott produced a certificate from Duck Creek Monthly Meeting. On 13/9/1751 Gershom Mott being removed out of the verge of our monthly meeting requested a certificate for himself and wife. On 14/10/1761. Gresham Mott produced a certificate to this meeting for himself and four children: Joshua, John, William and Sarah. On 11/11/1764 it was reported that Gresham Mott had taken a wife contrary to the rules of our discipline. On 12/12/1764 Gresham Mott was disowned. On 9/3/1768 Gersham Mott condemned his misconduct. On 8/6/1768 it was discussed that Gersham Mott might be received into Unity again.

12/4/1751. Joseph Thraul applies for a certificate.

8/1/1752. Abraham Milton and Mary Jones [m. 12/2/1752] and John Newell and Martha Collins declared their intentions of marriage [m. 12/2/1752].

11/3/1752. Joshua Lamb and Susanna Corse declared their intentions of marriage. [They m. 8/4/1752.]

13/5/1752. James Claypole having made a breach in our discipline by taking a wife not of our Society and this being his second disorder of this kind. On 8/7/1752 James Claypole produced a letter of condemnation.

13/5/1752. James Dunkan has taken a wife not of our Society.

10/6/1752. William Rasin has made a breach in discipline by taking the oaths to the Government in order to qualify himself for a legislative member. On 8/11/1752 William Rasin, son of Thomas and Mary Rasin, was disowned.

10/6/1752. Whereas it hath been made to appear that Stephen Brown is the father of a base born child he is expected to give answer for his disorderly conduct.

8/7/1752. Oliver Caulk having an intention of marriage with a woman not within the verge of our monthly meeting made application for a certificate.

12/8/1752. Stephen Brown has left the Province and gone to Carolina.

11/10/1752. John Corse having taken a wife who is not of our Society, he is expected to condemn his disorder. On 11/4/1753 it was reported that John Corse is the father of a base born child of a woman near Duck Creek and was outgoing in his marriage. The meeting notes on 9/5/1753 the John Corse refuses to appear at the monthly meeting. On 13/6/1753 John Corse was disowned.

11/4/1753. Writson Browning and Sarah Vansant declared their intentions of marriage. [They m. 9/5/1753.]

11/4/1753. James Dunkan produced a letter of condemnation, having taken a wife of another profession.

11/4/1753. There is a difference subsisting between David Hull and George Rasin about some accompts. On 13/3/1754 George Rasin produced a letter condemning his disorderly opposing David Hull.

9/5/1753. Southy Miflin and Johannah Thomas declared their intentions of marriage. [They m. 13/6/1753.]

10/7/1753. Thomas Browning produced a certificate from East Nottingham Monthly Meeting.

5/8/1753. Stephen Gudgion produced a few lines from Cecil Meeting and is taken under the care of Friends.

15/4/1754. George Dunkan having become an object of charity and in want of apparel the meeting will get him some necessaries.

8/5/1754. John Gale having lately been guilty of drinking to excess is to be dealt with love and a report made to the next monthly meeting.

12/6/1754. The woman has acquitted John Corsey in writing. On 10/7/1754 John Corse was disowned.

11/9/1754. Francis Spearman having lately been guilty of drinking to excess, to be dealt with in love. On 11/6.1755 Francis Spearman produced a letter condemning his drinking to excess.

9/10/1754. Morgan Brown being removed out of this Province sent a request to our monthly meeting for a certificate.

13/11/1754. Nathaniel Cleaves requests to be taken under the care of Friends.

14/5/1755. John Gale produces his letter condemning his disorderly walking (drinking too freely).

14/5/1755. Henry Coventry was appointed to speak with Nathan Wright to be known of him whether or not he is desirous to be under the care of Friends. On 14/4/1756 it was reported that Nathan Wright did not seem inclinable to condemn his disorder.

14/5/1755. The monthly meeting book is put into the hands of Abraham Milton to transcribe.

9/7/1755. Pearse Lamb having been charged by Elisebeth Corse on oath of being the father of her base born child and he denying the same the meeting appoints David Hull, Samuel Walace, Joshua Vanzant and Tho: Bower to make a report. On 11/2/1756 Pearse Lamb was disowned.

10/9/1755. Thos. Gilpin by a Friend produced a certificate to this meeting.

12/11/1755. John George about to take a wife within the verge of Talbot Co. Monthly Meeting requests a certificate on that account.

10/3/1756. Bathia Wiat wife of James Wiat requested to be taken under the notice of Friends.

12/5/1756. Francis Lamb has gone out in marriage and also disguised himself with strong liquor as not to be able to deport himself which he condemns. On 9/2/1757 Francis Lamb condemned his taking a wife by a hireling priest and by drinking strong liquors to excess.

14/7/1756. Elisebeth Course now Hart having gone out from Friends by disorderly walking. On 9/12/1756 Elizabeth Corse now Hart was disowned, having taken a husband out of the unity of Friends.

14/7/1756. Nathan Cleaves's life has been distinguished by many ill practices. On ?/10/1756 Nathaniel Cleaves was disowned.

11/8/1756. At this meeting we received advice from the Quarterly Meeting to make up a testification against Daniell Hull that was published against him in Talbot Co.

11/8/1756. David Course produced a certificate from Friends in Philadelphia.

?/10/1756. George Lamb and Sarah George declared their intentions of marriage. [They m. 10/11/1756.]

*13/11/1756. Henry Bodien and Hannah Hull declared their intentions of marriage. On 14/1/1757 it was reported that the marriage of Henry Bodien and Hannah Hull had been completed in good order.

9/12/1756. John Gale continues his practice of drinking to excess.

13/4/1757. Received a line of recommendation from East Nottingham Monthly Meeting on account of Jonathan White.

8/6/1757. Richard Hosier has brought reproach on truth from his disorderly marriage and other disorderly practices. Thomas Masling and Joseph George have brought reproach by disorderly marriages.

13/7/1757. Daniel Hull disowned, having contracted many debts which were beyond his power and ability to comply with.

10/8/1757. James Claypool condemns his disorderly practices, having taken a wife by a priest.

10/8/1757. Joseph Garrett now deceased.

10/8/1757. Thomas Masling condemns his disorderly practice.

14/9/1757. Prince Snow guilty of indecent behaviour. On ?/12/1757 Thomas Browning complained that Prince Snow is indebted to him and does not pay. On 9/8/1758 Prince Snow condemned his former conduct. On 9/9/1761 a complaint was made against Prince Snow that he has several debts which he neglects to pay. On 9/12/1761 Prince Snow was disowned.

18/10/1757. Daniel B— produced a certificate on himself and wife from Wilmington Monthly Meeting.

18/10/1757. Daniel Corse and Mary Bowers declared their intentions of marriage. [They m. 9/11/1757.]

9/11/1757. Richard Hosier condemns his outgoing in marriage.

9/11/1757. Mary Covington (Coventry) was disowned.

9/11/1757. Cooter(?) Griffith desires to be brought under the care of Friends.

?/12/1757. Henry Brooks condemns his former misconduct (marrying by a priest).

?12/1757. Robert Clothier and Rebecka Simonds declared their intentions of marriage. [They m. 1/12/1758 at Sassafrax Meeting House.]

8/3/1758/ James Tibbitt has married out and abuses himself with strong liquor. On 9/8/1758 James Tibbett condemned his former behaviour (taking a wife by a priest and drinking hard liquor to excess).

12/4/1758. Sassafras Meeting applies for a certificate for Jonathan White.

?/5/1758. Received certificate for Joseph Gill.

9/8/1758. A certificate was received for George Gilpin.

7/11/1758. A certificate for Pearse (?) Bowers prepared.

19/12/1758. A certificate was received from Tho: Goodman(?) and Tho: Chartown.

14/2/1759. A certificate was produced for Daniel Barns (?) and wife.

14/2/1759. Emanuel Jenkins [Jenkinson] and Martha Bowers declared their intentions of marriage. [They m. 14/3/1759.]

14/2/1759. James Kelly requests to be taken under the care of Friends.

14/2/1759. Christopher Vansant will transcribe for the meeting in place of Abraham Milton.

14/3/1759. Received a few lines from Duck Creek Monthly Meeting recommending Johnathan Barras.

9/5/1759. Jonathan White condemns his disorder in drinking to excess.

13/6/1759. A Friend from Little Creek desires a certificate for Rebeckah Bostick who formerly resided within the verge of our monthly meeting and now within the verge of their monthly meeting (she being but a child while in this area).

13/6/1759. Daniel Jackson produced a certificate from Wilmington Monthly Meeting for himself, wife and brother-in-law Joseph Warner.

8/8/1759. James Welch has lately been guilty of abusive behaviour amongst his neighbours.

12/12/1759. Joseph George condemned his disorderly marriage, having taken a wife by a hireling priest.

12/12/1759. Edmund Carter condemned his disorderly marriage.

13/2/1760. William Gudgeon and Mary Snow declared their intentions of marriage. [They m. 17/3/1760.]

12/3/1760. James Welch condemns his former conduct.

12/3/1760. Henry Thomas will be visited to inform him that Friends expect him to condemn his disorderly marriage. On 14/5/1760 Henry Thomas condemned his disorderly marriage, having taken a wife by a hireling priest.

14/5/1760. This meeting appoints Henry Bodien to transcribe in the meeting book - and this meeting appoints Thomas Bowers and Henry Bodien to peruse the entries to see which may be left out and not recorded.

13/8/1760. Joseph Gill sometime ago produced a certificate to this meeting which was mislaid and should have been recommended to Talbot County Monthly Meeting on account of marriage.

11/2/1761. A certificate for Jonathan White was produced.

11/2/1761. A certificate was requested for Joseph Warner.

10/5/1761. John Vansant requested a certificate on his conduct and clearness of marriage ingagements.

12/8/1761. Samuel Wallis produced a paper condemning his disorderly marriage, having married by a hireling priest.

12/8/1761. Abraham Milton has contracted several large debts which he is unable to pay. On 10/11/1762 Abraham Milton was disowned.

9/9/1761. Michael Corse has taken a wife of another persuasion and married by a hireling priest and has declined attending meetings.

9/9/1761. Jonathan Neal produced a certificate from Talbot County Monthly Meeting.

9/9/1761. Samuel Wallis acquainted the meeting that he had 600 lbs. of tobacco executed [meaning confiscated?] for —? wagons.

14/10/1761. At this meeting was read a testimony against William Isaacs (?) and his wife from Philadelphia Monthly Meeting on account of getting married by a hireling priest.

10/2/1762. A certificate was received from Darby Monthly Meeting in Chester Co., Pennsylvania, for Thomas Canby, wife Sarah and son Nathaniel Canby.

10/2/1762. It is reported that John Lamb hath been guilty of begetting a base born child and behaving indecently at the marriage of the young woman to another man. On 9/6/1762 John Lamb condemned his behavior.

10/3/1762. Michael Corse, son of Michael Corse, was disowned having taken a wife of another persuasion and married by a hireling priest and has declined attending our religious meetings.

10/3/1762. Robert George condemns his disorderly marriage.

10/3/1762. Benjamin Barry made application in regard to Henry Wallis, son of Samuel Wallis, who had been bound to him. The boy has left him.

12/5/1762. Jonathan Neal having moved to Talbot Co. requests a certificate.

11/8/1762. There is a difference between Joshua Vansant and Ridson Browning.

8/9/1762. William Warner produced a certificate on himself and child.

8/9/1762. Thomas Bowers produced a paper condemning his disorderly marriage.

8/9/1762. A complaint was received that Samuel Thomas has married a woman of another persuasion. On 8/6/1763 Samuel Thomas was disowned.

8/9/1762. A complaint was made that Isaac Milton's widow has neglected to send her children to meetings. On 10/11/1762 Ann Milton states that she considers her children too young except for one to attend meetings.

13/10/1762. Nathan Nowland produced a certificate for himself, wife and three children from Chester Monthly Meeting at Providence, Pennsylvania.

8/12/1762. Friends are attempting to resolve differences between Joshua Vansant and Thomas Gilpin, and between Joshua Vansant and Writson Browning.

8/12/1762. Henry Brooks by his last will and testament directed that his children after the death of his wife would be educated by the Quakers of Cecil Monthly Meeting. His widow has died and has not fully administered the estate.

9/2/1763. Benjamin Jacobs produced a certificate from Gwynedd Monthly Meeting, Pennsylvania.

9/2/1763. Robert Evans will be questioned as to why he has not produced a certificate, having lived within the verge of this monthly meeting for several years, Friends understanding that he has a certificate which he has not produced. On 8/6/1763 Robert Evans condemned his behavior.

13/4/1763. Reported that Abraham Milton, son of Isaac Milton and James George have taken wives by a hireling priest. [Disowned]

13/7/1763. Abraham Rasin condemned his disorderly marriage.

13/7/1763. A certificate is produced for William Warner, Junr., from Wilmington Monthly Meeting.

13/7/1763. Thomas Gilpin having removed to Philadelphia, requests a certificate. On 14/9/1763 those preparing a certificate for Thomas Gilpin noted that there are some unsettled matters. On 8/2/1764 it was reported that obstacles in the case of Thomas Gilpin's certificate had been removed.

10/8/1763. Robert Evans condemns his marrying a woman not of the Society by a hireling priest.

14/9/1763. The meeting received a testimony against Hannah Warner.

14/9/1763. In a meeting with William Warner, Junr., he states that the report that he is the father of a base born child is groundless but that he has gone out in marriage. On 9/5/1764 Writson Browning acknowledged that his conversation with William Warner were too warm and that he believed that the scandalous reports on William Warner were false.

14/9/1763. It was reported that George Gilpin has commenced a suit in the court of chancery against Joshua Vansant.

9/11/1763. Informed that Joseph Gill is guilty of frequently drinking to excess and committing other disorders.

11/4/1764. Received a certificate from Nottingham Monthly Meeting for Pearce Bowers signifying his membership and clearness in marriage.

11/4/1764. Ann Bowers, wife of Thomas Bowers, Junr., appeared at Cecil Meeting 8th of 9th mo., 1762 and requested to be taken under Friends' notice and the meeting agreed to receive her, her life and conversations being agreeable to Friends. [*Why is this entered two years later?*]

11/4/1764. William Warner produced a certificate from Wilmington Monthly Meeting for himself, wife and three children; Benjamin, Samuel and Daniel Warner.

9/5/1764. Received a denial from the Women's meeting against Hanah Corse now Layburn for marrying by a priest.

9/5/1764. It was reported that George Lamb has got married by a hireling priest. On 8/8/1764 he was disowned.

9/5/1764. It was reported that John Corse has given way to passion and beaten a man with a stick.

9/5/1764. There is a complaint against Pierce Bowers that he neglects attending meetings and drinks to excess and is consumed in making of horse races.

11/7/1764. It was reported that Robert George hath been buying of a Negro.

8/8/1764. Rebeccah Corse, now Lamb, disowned, having gotten married by a hireling priest.

12/9/1764. Samuel Wallis Junr is appointed overseer in stead of James Wiatt, deceased, at Cecil Meeting.

12/9/1764. Sassafras Meeting reports that Benjamin Jacobs hath removed and requests a certificate.

10/10/1764. Susannah Bentham produced a paper condemning her disorderly conduct.

10/10/1764. The publication of Elizabeth Tilden's condemnation of her misconduct in going out in marriage being omitted it will be made publick at the close of first day meeting.

10/10/1764. Jane Clother now Vickers is disowned, having gone to a priest to take a husband.

10/10/1764. Pearce Bowers of Kent Co. is disowned, having neglected the attendance of meeting for worship and being overtaken in strong drink and encouraging horse racing.

10/10/1764. The women Friends produced the denial of Hannah Bordley and Mary Rasin on account of their disorderly marriages.

9/1/1765. Henry Bodien who hath been indisposed is replaced as clerk by John Vansant at present.

13/2/1765. James Maslin, having removed, requests a certificate. On 8/5/1765 it was reported that matters still obstruct the preparation of the certificate for James Maslin.

10/4/1765. Thomas Bowers complains that at this time Joshua Vansant is at variance with his wife. On 12/6/1765 the meeting noted that Joshua Vansant and his wife have been encouraged to cohabit. At the same meeting it was reported that Joshua Vansant has been guilty of attending other places of worship, dancing, gambling and keeping —? company. On 10/7/1765 Issabella Vansant, wife of Joshua Vansant, had not offered any satisfaction to this meeting. On 9/10/1765 Joshua Vansant, Junr., Kent Co., was disowned, having gotten into the practice of dancing and gaming and declining the attendance of our meetings for worship. On 11/7/1774. Joshua Vansant acknowledged his past misconduct. On 14/12/1774 it was thought that the conduct of Joshua Vansant was such as may recommend him to the notice of Friends.

10/4/1765. John Corse condemns his behaviour.

10/4/1765. Ann Milton, now Delahunty is disowned for taking a husband by a hireling priest.

10/4/1765. Sary (Sarah) George, now Simmons, is disowned for taking a husband by a hireling priest.

8/5/1765. Testimony received against Mary Canby from the Women's Meeting.

12/6/1765. Mary Canby of Cecil Co. disowned, she having had a child unlawfully(?) and neglected our religious meetings.

12/6/1765. Lewis Clothier requests a certificate on his clearness of marriage, to be directed to Nottingham Monthly Meeting.

10/7/1765. David Corse by way of Cecil Meeting requests a certificate regarding his clearness in marriage, to be directed to Talbot Co. Monthly Meeting..

14/8/1765. There is a complaint against Thomas Maslin, Junr., for his going out in marriage. On 12/2/1766Thomas Maslin, Junr. was disowned, having taken a wife of another persuasion and gone to a priest to accomplish his marriage.

14/8/1765. Chester Meeting reports that Joseph Brown is supposedly the father of a base born child.

14/8/1765. Sassafras Meeting offers a complaint against William Gudgeon and William Warner for their neglect of attending meetings.

9/10/1765. Thomas Bowers, Junr., and John Lamb have acknowledged buying slaves.

9/10/1765. A certificate was received from Wilmington for Benjamin Canby, wife and child.

13/11/1765. Those appointed to treat with James Maslin report that he promises to attend the next monthly meeting - the young woman by whom he hath had a child will be visited. On 12/2/1766 the young woman by whom James Maslin had a child says that he promised her marriage and hath not made her satisfaction. On 9/7/1766 James Maslin was disowned. On 11/11/1772 James Maslin condemned his misconduct for which he was disowned and expressed a desire to come under the care of Friends.

11/12/1765. Henry Bodien and Margaret Wallis declared their intentions of marriage. [They m. 9/1/1760.]

8/1/1766. Standing elders appointed for Cecil Meeting: Thomas Bowers, Samuel Wallis and Sarah Rasin; Joshua Lamb was appointed overseer in place of Thomas Bowers.

8/1/1766. George Lamb acknowledged having purchased a Negro owing to his not being acquainted that it was contrary to discipline.

12/2/1766. Joseph Brown is disowned; he pays for the maintenance of a base born child of which it is reported he is the father.

3/12/1766. William Warner is disowned, having neglected attending meetings and hath got into the practice of gameing.

3/12/1766. William Gudgeon is disowned, having neglected attending meetings and hath got into the practice of gameing.

9/4/1766. George Lamb condemns his taking a wife by a hireling priest.

14/5/1766. Pheby Dunkin now Powel, is disowned for having taken a husband by a hireling priest.

11/6/1766. A Friend from Chester Meeting acquaints the meeting that two of Isaac Melton's youngest children are destitute of homes, their mother being dead. John Smith is appointed to secure such part of the estate as is to be got and get good places for the children and render an account thereof.

13/8/1766. Sassafrass Meeting offers a complaint against George Gilpin in that he hath neglected attending meetings and given way to lust as Sarah Cunningham has charged him with being the father of her child unlawfully begotten. On 10/12/1766. George Gilpin was disowned.

10/9/1766. Cecil Meeting offers a complaint against John Lamb for having so far given to lust as Sarah Miller charges him with being the father of her child unlawfully begotten. On 11/3/1767 John Lamb was disowned.

8/10/1766. Friends have found a suitable place to board Isaac Melton so as to school him.

8/10/1766. Samuel Wallis being appointed to inspect the minutes, being dead, his son Samuel Wallis is appointed in his stead.

?/11/1766. Testimony against Elisabeth Melton now King concerning her going out in marriage.

?/11/1766. A certificate is received from Wilmington Monthly Meeting for James Warner.

?/11/1766. Sassafrass Meeting complains against Robert Evans, he having neglected attending meetings and followed gameing and hath taken an oath.

10/12/1766. George Browning requests a certificate to Third Haven Monthly Meeting signifying his clearness of marriage engagements.

11/2/1767. The Friend is removed by death who was appointed to take the care of Henry Brooke's children and to their estates. Samuel Wallis and Abraham Rasin will inspect into the circumstances of the children and their estates.

11/3/1767. The executors of the estate of Henry Bodien are willing to give up the children of Henry Brookes with their estates, first having sufficient bonds.

11/3/1767. David Corse having removed some distance from this meeting, Abraham Rasin is appointed collector in his stead.

8/4/1767. Cecil Meeting has offered a complaint against James Dunkin, he lately having purchased a Negro slave.

13/6/1767. A certificate was received for Elisabeth Corse from Third Haven Monthly Meeting.

8/7/1767. Isaac Whitelock produced a few lines by way of a certificate from the meeting to which he belongs. [Lancaster Co., Pennsylvania] On 8/7/1767 Isaac Whitelock and Sarah Rasin declared their intentions of marriage. [They m. 8/7/1767.]

12/8/1767. Sassafrass Preparative Meeting offers a complaint against Daniel Jackson for having neglected attending of meetings.

14/10/1767. A testification against Elizabeth Gale [now Moore] made on account of her taking a husband by a hireling priest.

11/11/1767. Informed that Isaac Milton's board and schooling is nearly due.

11/11/1767. Robert George requests a certificate, to be directed to Third Haven Monthly Meeting on account of marriage.

9/12/1767. A testification was made against Mary Trew now Hastings on account of going out in marriage.

15/1/1768. A certificate was requested for Joshua Mott, being put an apprentice to a Friend in Pennsylvania.

10/2/1768. Daniel Jackson has moved away in a disorderly manner whereby his sureties for debt are liable to suffer.

10/2/1768. Abraham Rasin complains that David Corse delays paying his last demand against him. On 9/3/1768 David Corse says he will attempt to make satisfaction.

10/2/1768. Sassafras Meeting requests a certificate for Benjamin Canby, wife and children [to Wilmington Monthly Meeting]. On 15/7/1768 the meeting notes that regarding the certificate for Benjamin Canby and his family there appears to be some matters unsettled and he has gone to sea.

15/7/1768. A certificate received from Philadelphia for Samuel Moiton, Junr.

15/7/1768. Sassafras Meeting requests a certificate for John Booth(?) to be directed to Duck Creek Monthly Meeting.

15/7/1768. A request was received from Rebeckah Hosier informing that Henry Thomas and his wife both are dead and have left two small children which she desires to be guardian to. The meeting concurs.

6/4/1768. Reported that Daniel Jackson is in confinement and not in the verge of Wilmington Monthly Meeting.

6/4/1768. Testification against Elizabeth Tilden for marrying out.

11/5/1768. Testification against Margaret Boudeen now Rasin for marrying out.

11/5/1768. The Women Friends having requested of this meeting to have the two young children of Henry Brooks put to school at Wilmington and inform likewise they have provided two suitable places, viz., Zachariah Ferrises or Hester Whites.

8/6/1768. A certificate for John Bostick was prepared.

8/6/1768. Testification against Bethias Milbourn now Penington on account of her outgoing in marriage.

8/6/1768. George Browning is appointed clerk.

5/10/1768. Testification is to be made against Daniel Jackson.

5/10/1768. Lewis Clother requests a certificate on account of marriage to be directed to Nottingham Monthly Meeting.

9/11/1768. Sassafras Meeting informs that Guy Snow has taken a wife contrary to our discipline.

9/11/1768. Slaves of Isaac Whitelock are to be set free: Mary to be free from this date; Dick, Toney, Grace, on 1st da., 1st mo., 1770; and Jacob, Ruth, Aby,

Sampson, Tom, James, Rachel, Hannah and Easter, when they shall severally arrive to the age of 24, and their ages are as followeth: Jacob, 16; Ruth, 17; Tom, 6; Rachel, 2; James, 20th of 11th mo., 2 years; Hannah, 6 mos. From 10th mo., 1768; Easter, 1 month from the date above mentioned.

11/1/1769. Testification was made against Haraminty Brooks now Rasin on account of going out in marriage.

8/2/1769. Testification was made against Bersheba Howel for her outgoing in marriage.

8/2/1769. John Stuart and Rebecah Hosier declared their intentions of marriage, he belonging to another monthly meeting. [Anne Arundel Co.] [They m. 9/3/1769.]

8/3/1769. Sassafras Meeting reports that Nathan Newland is accused by Ann Berry of getting two base born children, they both born at one birth, and that he has since gone out in marriage with another woman.

8/3/1769. Lewis Clother requests a certificate of removal to Nottingham Monthly Meeting.

12/4/1769. Robert Greaves produced a certificate from the Philadelphia Monthly Meeting.

12/4/1769. A certificate of removal is requested for Anne Rasin to be directed to the Sadsbury Monthly Meeting.

10/5/1769. Complaint against Henry Wallice on account of his outgoing in marriage.

10/5/1769. Complaint against William Bowers for buying a slave.

10/5/1769. Chester Meeting reports that John Pope requests a certificate of removal to be directed to Burlington Monthly Meeting.

14/6/1769. William Bowers does not set any time for the freedom of his slave.

9/8/1769. A certificate was prepared for Benjamin Canby, his wife Susannah and children: Thomas and Deborough.

9/8/1769. Cecil Meeting thinks it advisable to remove Samuel Wallice from the station of overseer, as he seems to decline the attendance of meetings.

13/9/1769. John Stewart produced a certificate of removal from Third Haven Monthly Meeting.

8/11/1769. Women Friends recommend Hannah Warner to the notice and care of Friends.

10/1/1770. Chester Meeting offers that Edward Comegys has taken a wife of another persuasion and by a hireling priest.

10/1/1770. The meeting is uneasy in regard to the manner of Sophia Brooks being educated.

14/2/1770. Testification against William Bowers was given to his brother, Thomas Bowers, to give to him.

14/2/1770. Testification against Martha Comegys now Whales on account of her outgoing in marriage.

14/2/1770. A complaint from Sassafras Meeting that James Welch has married out.

11/4/1770. Robert Greaves requests a certificate of removal.

16/6/1770. Joseph Canby produced a certificate from Philadelphia Monthly Meeting.

12/9/1770. Testification against Mary Milton now Brown on account of her marrying out.

12/12/1770. Informed that Bartlett George and Abraham Rasin have married out. On 8/4/1772 Abraham Rasin condemned his disorderly marriage.

12/12/1770. A certificate will be prepared for John Corse on account of marriage.

12/12/1770. Testification against Hannah Melton now George.

8/5/1771. Phebe Newland produced a certificate to this meeting for herself and daughter Phebe Offley from Duckcreek Monthly Meeting held at Little Creek in Kent County on Delaware.

12/6/1771. Henry Troth, Junr., produced a certificate to this meeting from Third Haven Monthly Meeting.

12/6/1771. Chester Meeting informs that Jessy and Bartice Comegys who removed sometime past from amongst us desire to have a certificate, directed to Thirdhaven Monthly Meeting.

11/9/1771. Samuel Wallis condemns his marrying out.

9/10/1771. Testification against Anne Wallice on account of her getting married by a priest. On 3/12/1773 Ann Wallice condemned her marrying by a priest.

13/11/1771. Those appointed some time past by their meeting to have the care and oversight of Mary Rasin, report they think her life and conversation is such as may recommend her to the notice of Friends again.

11/12/1771. A certificate was received from Deer Creek Monthly Meeting for Cassandra Corse.

11/12/1771. John Corse requests a certificate of removal for his brother Thomas Corse.

8/1/1772. John Fargason has a desire to be joined in unity among Friends.

8/7/1772. Testification against Mary Page, she having gone out in marriage.

8/7/1772. To treat with Hannah Brooks, she having sold a slave.

9/9/1772. Joseph Canby handed a certificate for Thomas Wilson from Wilmington Monthly Meeting.

9/9/1772. Joseph Canby requested a certificate, to be directed to Wilmington Monthly Meeting on account of marriage with a young woman of that meeting.

9/12/1772. William Trew requests a certificate, to be directed to Third Haven Monthly Meeting on account of marriage.

13/1/1773. A complaint was made against John Vansant on account of his not conducting himself uprightly towards his creditors in Philadelphia. On 11/3/1773 the monthly meeting concluded that the affair with John Vansant was ended, he being dead.

11/3/1773. Testification against Isabelah Vansant now Palmer, she having neglected religious meetings and married out.

11/3/1773. Thomas Nock and Mary Caulk declared their intentions of marriage, he being a member of another meeting. On 12/5/1773 Thomas Nock produced a certificate from Duck Creek Monthly Meeting. [Thomas Nock, Jr. of Kent Co. on Delaware, and Mary Caulk of Cecil Co., m. at Sassafrass meeting House on 13/5/1773.]

12/5/1773. A certificate was received from Wilmington Monthly Meeting for Hannah Canby.

12/5/1773. A certificate was requested on behalf of Sarah Browning for her son Joshua who is put an apprentice at Duck Creek.

9/6/1773. Gersham Mott in behalf of his son John requests a certificate, to be directed to Duck Creek Monthly Meeting.

9/6/1773. An uneasiness subsists between Joseph and Robert George concerning a division of their land which was left by their grandfather's will.

9/6/1773. It was reported that William Trew has bought a Negro slave and has since taken a wife by a hireling priest.

11/8/1773. Elizabeth Devenport produced a certificate from Duck Creek Monthly Meeting.

8/9/1773. Samuel Norton desires a certificate of removal.

10/11/1773. A certificate was received from Wilmington Monthly Meeting for Susannah Newland.

12/1/1774. Testification was made against Hannah Brooks now Hurt who hath sold a Negro slave and married a man not of our persuasion by a priest.

12/1/1774. Samuel Wallice condemns his misconduct.

12/1/1774. William Janney produced a certificate from Duck Creek Monthly Meeting.

12/1/1774. David Jones requests a certificate, to be directed to Abington Monthly Meeting.

9/2/1774. Testification was made against Rebeccah Comegys on account of her going out in marriage.

9/2/1774. A certificate was received from Sadsbury Monthly Meeting for George Rasin.

13/4/1774. Division of land for Robert and Joseph George has been completed. [*Metes and bounds are given in the minutes*.]

11/5/1774. Having not mentioned Jane Vansant's daughter Rachel's name in her mother's certificate to Duck Creek Monthly Meeting, it is ordered that a certificate be sent to that meeting in her regard.

8/6/1774. Samuel Wallis's conduct favorably recommends him to the notice of Friends again.

8/6/1774. Testification was made against Sophia Brooks now Wallis.

8/6/1774. Thomas Wilson has removed to Philadelphia and requests a certificate.

14/9/1774. Cecil Meeting complains against John Ferguson on account of his being guilty of fighting with another man. On 12/10/1774 John Ferguson condemned his misconduct.

14/12/1774. Testification was made against Henry Troth.

14/12/1774. Testification was made against Elizabeth now Troth on account of marrying her 1st cousin and accomplishing this by a hireling priest.

8/2/1775. The Women Friends offered Susannah Lamb and Rebecca Lamb for Cecil and Ann George and Rebecca Stuart for Chester as our ... of their respective meetings.

?/3/1773. Susannah Maslin was recommended for membership.

10/5/1775. Our clerk being dead the meeting appoints Abraham Reason in his stead.

10/5/1775. John Berry and Margaret Melton declared their intentions of marriage. On 14/6/1775 John Berry produced a certificate regarding his clearness in marriage. [John Berry, son of Joseph Berry of Talbot Co., and Margaret Milton, daughter of Abraham Milton of Kent Co., m. at Chester Meeting House on 14/6/1775.]

14/6/1775. Testification was made against Hannah Wallis now Mansfield on account of her marrying out.

14/6/1775. Abel Janey produced a certificate from Duck Creek Monthly Meeting.

13/9/1775. Solomon Dawson produced a certificate from Duck Creek Monthly Meeting for himself and wife.

13/9/1775. Women Friends produced a certificate for Margaret Berry.

10/1/1776. William Rasin has married by the assistance of a priest. Disowned.

10/1/1776. Gershom Mott stands in need of some assistance.

14/2/1776. Joseph Wilkeson produced a certificate of removal from Wilmington and his wife Mary produced one from New Garden Monthly Meeting.

13/3/1776. Chester Meeting has a complaint against Jesse Comegys and Gideon Comegys for their neglecting attendance of meetings, and bearing arms to learn the art of War.

I Sarah Rasin now of the Borough of Wilmington, New Castle Co., do set free from bondage my Negro boy named John when he shall arrive at the age of 21 years which will be about the 30th da. of the 12th mo., 1780. Dated 16/5/1776.

10/4/1776. Chester Meeting offers a complaint against James Smyth for neglecting religious meetings and in the practice of training in the military service to learn the art of War. On 8/9/1779 James Smyth produced an acknowledgment of his outgoing. On 8/12/1779. James Smyth condemned his joining in military service; also gaming. and ...? conversations of the world.

8/5/1776. Sassafras Meeting complains that John Browning is in the practice of training to learn the art of War.

12/6/1776. Cecil Meeting reports that Joseph Cutter desires to be taken under the care of Friends.

12/6/1776. Thomas Coarse produced a certificate of removal from New Garden Monthly Meeting.

14/8/1776. Complaint against George Raisin and Malikia Gale that were in the practice of bearing arms and neglecting the attendances of religious meetings. On 10/11/1776 Malaichi Gale was disowned.

14/8/1776 Pierce Lamb condemns his past misconduct. On 9/7/1777 he was received into membership.

7/9/1776. Testification against Rebecca Wilkison.

9/10/1776. Cecil Meeting reports that William Moss desires to be taken under the care of Friends.

9/10/1776. A certificate of removal is requested for Joseph Comegys to Philadelphia.

11/12/1776. Solomon Dawson requested a certificate to Third Haven Monthly Meeting showing his clearness from marriage engagements.

3/4/1777. Gershom Mott does not stand in need except for the education of his children.

3/4/1777. Manumissions are now recorded in a separate book.

9/7/1777. William Mott having been incautiously drawn into the spirit of war has offered a written acknowledgment condemning his misconduct.

9/7/1777. Lydia Dawson produced a certificate of removal from Third Haven Monthly Meeting.

9/7/1777. Solomon Dawson replaces previous clerk who was removed by death.

13/8/1777. Richard Milton produced a certificate of removal from Third Haven Monthly Meeting.

10/9/1777. Samuel Wallis is appointed treasurer.

10/9/1777. Cecil Meeting complains that John Wallis and William Wyat neglect attending meetings and for acting in military service. On 11/3/1778 both were disowned.

10/9/1777. Cecil Meeting complains against John Ferguson for moving outside the verge of this monthly meeting without requesting a certificate; left his affairs unsettled, and has been employed as overseer of slaves - also neglects the attendances of meetings. On 11/3/1778 he was disowned.

8/10/1777. Cecil Meeting offers that George Williamson expresses a desire to be taken under the care of Friends.

8/10/1777. Chester Meeting offers a complaint against Joseph George for his neglecting the attendance of meetings and hiring a man as a substitute to go to war.

8/10/1777. Women Friends handed a testification against Elizabeth Sylvair formerly Janey for marrying out. Disowned.

8/10/1777. A certificate was prepared for Rebecca Smyth to Talbot Monthly Meeting [Third Haven].

8/10/1777. Bartlet George condemned his outgoing in marriage.

10/12/1777. The sufferings of James Maslin were recorded.

14/1/1778. Sassafras Meeting informs that Jonathan Devenport requests to be taken under the care of Friends, he being educated and brought amongst them.

14/1/1778. Sufferings:
Taken from Pierce Lamb one mare and 20 sheep valued at £40 [later changed to 60]for a demand of £40.1 for a substitute by William Merit, Sheriff.
Taken from Samuel Wallis for nonassociation 1 beef valued at £8 for a demands of £5.
Came and brought 50 armed men with their officers and sold 6 of James Maslin's cows, 5 to John Williams and 1 to Joel Willis which they drove away. The said cows were valued at £36 [later changed to 90] which were taken at a demand of £40 for substitute money.
From Joseph Wilkerson one horse worth £45 [later changed to 120] for a demands of £30 for substitute money by Thomas Boyer, sub-sheriff.
Taken from Able Janey 800 weight of pork worth £14 [later changed to 40] for a demands of £30 to buy a substitute.

11/3/1778.
Taken from Bartlett George 2 mares valued at £45 for a demand of £37
Taken from John Corse one milch cow valued at £12 for a demand of £6
Taken from Samuel Wallis one beef steer valued at £20 for a demands of £5.
Taken from George Lamb a young beef steer valued at £8 for a demands of £3.16 (non-association money and priests' demands).

11/3/1778. Rebecca Brown manumitted two Negroes, one to be free at proper age, the other at her death which appears to be all that she is possessed of except two elderly people who are hardly of capacity to support themselves whom she signified she would take care of during her time.

11/3/1778. Joseph George also being possessed of a number of slaves to discharge. On 13/5/1778 he was disowned.

11/3/1778. Robert George being appointed guardian for an orphan's estate in which there are several slaves whom he hath let go sometime past to act for themselves as free people except some minors.

11/3/1778. Ann Wilkins also having manumitted three, there being a number more in the family belonging to the children who are not yet arrived to age.

11/3/1778. Thos. Bowers has a number of slaves whom he seems determined not to release.

11/3/1778 Barsheba Gale having manumitted the one belonging to her, as also her two eldest daughters - each of them, one; the rest belonging to the young children and not likely to be released yet.

11/3/1778. It is believed that there are few other families that are but clear.

13/5/1778. Cecil Meeting complains against Thomas Bowers for deviating regarding the justification of war, and neglect of attending meetings. On 9/9/1778 he was disowned.

13/5/1778. Chester Meeting offers that Nicholas Brown desires to come under the care of Friends.

13/5/1778. Richard Millton has requested a certificate of removal to Third Haven Monthly Meeting.

13/5/1778. Susana Wilson produced a certificate from Duck Creek Monthly Meeting.

13/5/1778. Thomas Corse and Rosamond Lamb declared their intentions of marriage. [they m. 18/6/1778 at Cecil Meeting House.]

10/6/1778. Testimony against Sarah Story.

10/6/1778. Testimony against Mary Duire (Dwyer). On 8/7/1778 Mary Gale now Dwyer was disowned for marrying out.

10/6/1778. Mary Brown condemned her outgoing in marriage.

10/6/1778. Sassafras Meeting complains against Thos. Browning for neglecting attendance of meetings; also taking the test of the government and against George Browning for neglect of meetings and going to camp as a soldier.

10/6/1778. William Mott has gone out in marriage with a person not of the Society. On 12/8/1778 he was disowned.

8/7/1778. Chester Meeting requests a certificate for John Trew, to be directed to New Garden Monthly Meeting.

12/8/1778. Benjamin Dawson handed a certificate of removal from Duck Creek Monthly Meeting.

9/9/1778. Benjamin Dawson having removed, requests a few lines to Duck Creek Monthly Meeting.

9/9/1778. William Dawson, son of Benjamin Dawson of Duck Creek and Sarah Lamb, daughter of George Lamb, declared their intentions of marriage. [They m. 11/3/1779.]

9/9/1778. John Stewart was appointed clerk.

9/12/1778. Sassafras Meeting requests certificate of removal for Joshua Vansant, to be directed to Duck Creek Monthly Meeting.

14/4/1779. Cornelia Mitchell formerly Browning was disowned for marrying out.

12/5/1779. A certificate was produced for Sarah Dawson, directed to Duck Creek Monthly Meeting.

16/6/1779. Elizabeth Trew acknowledges her misconduct in selling a Negro and child; and expresses her willingness to redeem them if it ever should be in her power.

14/7/1779. William Moss requests that his children, Esther, William, Rebecca and Sarah, be taken under the care of Friends.

11/8/1779. Testimony against Elizabeth Vickars and Ann Parsons for their disorderly marriages.

11/8/1779. Mary Williamson, wife of George Williamson, desires to be taken under the notice of Friends.

13/10/1779. Chester Meeting requests assistance concerning a Negro which Ann George sold before marriage which is now in slavery, and her husband expressing a willingness to abide by the direction of Friends.

13/10/1779. Sassafras Meeting representatives request a few lines to New Garden Monthly Meeting for Samuel Martin who returned a certificate a few years back with ...?

13/10/1779. Samuel Troth produced a certificate of removal from Third Haven Monthly Meeting.

10/11/1779. William Dawson produced a certificate from Duck Creek Monthly Meeting for himself, wife and apprentice boy John Saunders.

8/12/1779. Thomas Corse replaces Solomon Dawson in assisting Samuel Wallis in transcribing the Monthly Meeting Book.

8/12/1779. A paragraph from the will of Abraham Rasin is read which places his son Warner Rasin under the care of Joshua Lamb, Thomas Bowers, Samuel

Wallis, and George Lamb until he arrives at the age of 21. Aforesaid trustees to rent, lease and receive rent on son's lands.

INDEX

www.ingramcontent.com/pod-product-compliance
Lightning Source LLC
LaVergne TN
LVHW012332100826
845148LV00017B/2126
9781680340167